C000314414

DÍARMAIT

KING OF LEINSTER

Mac Murchadas Ireland

LAIGIN Over-Kingdoms

Cairpre Sub-kingdoms and territories

UA BRIAIN Principal dynastic surnames

Ua Dubda Lesser dynastic surnames

Inis Eógain
Ua Nochartaig

UA MÁEL DORAIG
Cenél Conaill

Ciannachta
Ua Catháin

Uí Thuirte
Ua Flainn

MAC LOCHLAINN
Cenél Moen
Ua Gairmledaig

ULAID
Dál nAraide

Cenél nEógain
UA NÉILL
Cenél Feredaig

NORTHERN UÍ NÉILL

Fir Lurg

MacCana
Airthir
Ua hAnluain

MACDUINNSLEIBE
Dál Fiatach

Mac Cathmail

Uí Echach Coba

Cairpre

Fir Manach
Ua hÉicnig

Fir Manach

AIRGIALLA
Fernmag

Mac Óengusa

Uí Fiachrach Muaide
Ua Dubda

Uí Briúin
UA RUAIRC

Mag Luirg
Ua Máel Ruanaid

BREIFNE

UA CERBAILL

Uá Ragallaig

Machaire Gaileng

Gailenga
Ua hEgra

Luigne
Ua Gadra

Fir Umaill
Ua Máille

Brega
Ua Cellaig

CONNACT

Síl Muiredaig
MacRagnaill

Lóegaire
Ua Caindelbáin

Tara
Ua Congalaig

UA CONCHOBHAIR

Tethba
Uá Fergail

MIDE

Iarchonnacht
Ua Flaithbertaig

Ua Cellaig
Uí Maine

Delbna Ethra
MacCochláin

UA MÁELSECHNAILL

Fine Gall

Dublin

Uí Fiachrach Aldne
Ua hEidin

Síl nAnmicnada
Ua Matudáin

Uí Failge
Ua Conchobhair Failge

Uí Dúnchada
MacGilla Mocholmóc

Uí Fáelain
MacFáeláin

Corco Mruad
Ua Lochlainn

Ua Duinn

Ua Dimmussaig

Uí Máil

MacConmara
Dál Cais *UA BRIAIN*

Ua Cennétig

Loíges
Ua Morda

Uí Muiredaig
Ua Tuathail

LAIGIN

Osraige
Mac Gilla Pátraic

Fothairt
Ua Nualláin

TUADMUMU

Limerick

Éile
Ua Cerbaill

Uí Chennselaig

MACMURCHADA

Uí Chairpre
Ua Donnabáin

Ua Máel Riain

Ua Duibir

URMUMA

Uí Bairrche

Wexford

Corca Duibhne
Ua Failbe

Déise Muman
Ua Bric

Waterford

Ua Fáeláin

Uí Súillebáin

DESMUMU
MACCARTHAIG

Eóganacht Glenndamn
Ua Caím

Cork

Eóganacht Locha Léin
Ua Ségda
Ua Muirchertaig

Cenél Lóegaire
Ua Donnchada

Corco Loígde
Ua hEitircéoil

DIARMAIT

KING OF LEINSTER

NICHOLAS FURLONG

MERCIER PRESS

WHAT YOU NEED TO READ

MERCIER PRESS
Douglas Village, Cork
www.mercierpress.ie

Trade enquiries to Columba Mercier Distribution,
55a Spruce Avenue, Stillorgan Industrial Park, Blackrock, Dublin

© Nicholas Furlong, this edition 2006

1 85635 505 5

10 9 8 7 6 5 4 3 2 1

Mercier Press receives financial assistance from
the Arts Council/An Chomhairle Ealaíon

This book is sold subject to the condition that it shall not, by way of trade or
otherwise, be lent, resold, hired out or otherwise circulated without the publisher's
prior consent in any form of binding or cover other than that in which it is
published and without a similar condition being imposed on the subsequent
purchaser.

Printed in Ireland by ColourBooks Ltd

CONTENTS

Do Mairéad,
i gcuimhne ar na laetheanta a bhí

ACKNOWLEDGEMENTS

I wish to anticipate criticism by declaring the obvious. I am not a professional historian. What I have tried to do is to give as full and rounded a picture of Diarmait Mac Murchada as possible without burying him under the involved data of a long and complex reign. My dilemma was to accomplish this without the reader reaching confusion and chapter three at the same time.

The story is attempted from the Uí Chennselaig vantage point. Because the language I write in is not the language of the people involved I have found it better in a few cases to anglicise. I ask your forgiveness.

I am indebted to Donncha Ó Corráin of the Department of Mediaeval History, UCD, for early encouragement and the unveiling of what seemed to be the most hidden background in Diarmait Mac Murchada's life. For help cheerfully given, the writer is also indebted to a former teacher, Professor Tomás Ó Fiaich, St Patrick's College, Maynooth, and Professor John Ryan, S.J. Also to Ms Anna Drury and the staff of the Wexford County Library, the staff of the National Library, Dublin, the Royal Irish Academy, the Irish Central Library for Students, Trinity College Library and the Dominican Convent Library, Vienna. Thanks are also due to Dr Thomas Sherwood, St Peter's College, Wexford, for translation of documents from Latin; to Ricky Shannon, Brendan Hearne and Mairéad Furlong for many (and varied) suggestions, and lastly to Dan Nolan of Anvil Books whose unfailing injections of enthusiasm saw to it that the attempt on Diarmait Mac Murchada's life was made.

ACKNOWLEDGEMENTS
2006 EDITION

In the rewriting and updating for this edition I want to express my particular thanks to Dr Charles Doherty, Department of Early Irish History, UCD and Professor Francis John Byrne. I am also grateful to Elizabeth Fitzpatrick, NUIG; Dr Daniel Gahan, University of Evansville, Indiana; Dr Muriel McCarthy, Marsh's Library, Dublin; Børge Rønne, Virum, Denmark; Oireachtas Éireann; Jarlath Glynn and Celestine Rafferty of the Wexford County Library Service; Dr Margaret McCurtain, O.P.; Dr Billy Colfer, Slade; Bishop Laurence Ryan, Kildare and Leighlin; Dr Sean Mythen, Hilary Murphy, Angela Malone and Declan Moore for his work on the maps.

INTRODUCTION

Diarmait Mac Murchada, king of Uí Chennselaig, king of Leinster, king of the Norse, died at Ferns on 1 May 1171 after a reign of forty-six years. If, in the years after his death, he was allowed to rest in peace, this blessing was not permanent. In succeeding centuries, Ireland needed a scapegoat for defeat and for the defection of many of its ruling families. It needed to divert blame from the Church whose reforming zeal had welcomed intervention from overseas. There was a ready-made candidate to hand for this prosecution, Diarmait Mac Murchada.

By the 1600s popular feeling was summed up in the writings of the eminent Franciscan historians known to us as the Four Masters. Their obituary of Diarmait Mac Murchada suggested diabolical possession:

> *Diarmait Mac Murchada, king of Leinster, who had spread terror throughout Ireland, after putting the English in possession of the country, committing excessive evils against the Irish people, and plundering and burning many churches among which were Kells, Clonard and others, died this year of an intolerable and uncommon disease. He became putrid while living, by the miracles of God, through the intervention of Columcille, Finian and other saints of Ireland for having violated and plundered their churches. He died at Ferns, without making a will, without penance, without the Eucharist and without Extreme Unction, as his evil deeds deserved.*

In these days, three hundred years after that obituary, over eight hundred years after his death, the name of Diarmait Mac Murchada, anglicised to 'Dermot Mac Murrough', has been used in patriotic rhetoric in Dáil Éireann, at Dublin GPO rallies, and even in his own capital, Ferns, as synonymous with treachery and shame. The royal title to which he succeeded, king of Leinster, king of the foreigners – the Norse – has been abbreviated in his case so that he himself is referred to as 'Diarmait of the foreigners' as a term of abuse in which foreigners mean not the Norse, but the Normans and English. His image is so bad that there is a challenge to reverse the colour. The lesson of history, however, is that there is no black, no white; there are instead the many subtle shadings of motivation and circumstance.

Any objective examination of Diarmait Mac Murchada must absolve him of his current infamy. It is important that his life is examined, not with the wisdom of hindsight, but with an appreciation of the society with its political, religious and sexual currents, into which he was born. The other cultures familiar through geographic proximity must also be considered. And lastly his family circumstances must be taken into account. For Diarmait Mac Murchada was, through a series of four untimely deaths, elected to ruling power by his own people at the age of sixteen. If, on consideration of all these factors, the bar of history grants to Diarmait Mac Murchada an impartial hearing, his soul may be allowed to rest.

NICHOLAS FURLONG

The Uí Chennselaig Kings of Leinster up to 1171

The kings of Uí Chennselaig emerged from the dense mists of antiquity as ruling dynasts. The first king to be accepted as factually recorded was Enna Cennsalach who was also recognised as king of Leinster early in the fifth century A.D.

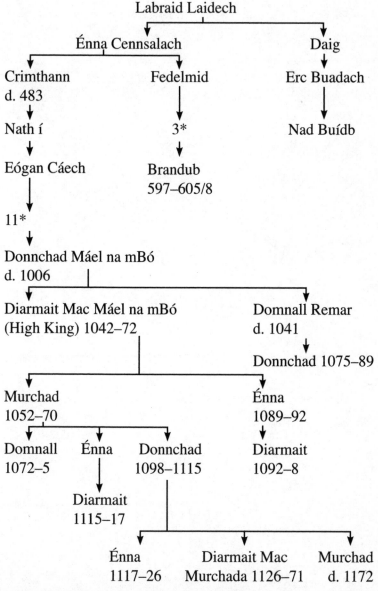

* = number of successions by kings other than the Mac Murchadas

ONE

The Inheritance

Brian Bóruma, king of Ireland, was killed by a retreating Norse soldier on the day of the victory of Clontarf, Good Friday 1014. He was one of the most gifted political rulers the country had ever seen.[1] His period of power ushered in an era of artistic and cultural achievement, which had been evolving for hundreds of years. He contributed something more significant than that, for he rose from an obscure territory to challenge and oust the Uí Néill ruling family hegemony of Ireland. Brian Bóruma set fire to ambition, for he demonstrated that any minor ruler, given opportunity, talent and men, could aspire to, and achieve, the highest power pinnacle in the land. After his death and celebrated victory, political chaos reigned in Ireland. For over 100 years afterwards, the ambitions of the lesser kings, stimulated by Brian Bóruma, erupted. Warfare filled the plains. Blinded hostages stumbled and fell. This gush of blood was to fulfil the tradition:

> *The land of Ireland is a sword land; let all men be challenged to show that there is any inheritance to the Island of Destiny except of conquest by din of battle.*[2]

Blood was spilled so that a lesser ruler could become a provincial king and a provincial king could become king of Ireland, claiming thereby a position of influence that was only as strong as the begrudged human being who achieved it.

This was the Ireland into which Diarmait Mac Donnchada Mac Murchada, the future king of Leinster and the Norse, was born in the year 1110. He was the third son of the reigning monarch of Leinster, Donnchadh Mac Murchada, and twentieth in descent from Énna Chennselaig, king of Leinster in the fifth century.[3]

If his fate, like Ireland's at the time, was to consist merely of interstate warfare, raids and burnings, his story would be very quickly told, but it was to be more complex. The centre of his world was at Rome and the web of his fate stretched in time back to the Roman Emperor Constantine, the founder of Byzantium, and was fraught with the political and spiritual conflict between two mighty powers of the day, the Holy Roman Catholic Church and the Holy Roman Empire. His future was to involve the Norse, Flemish, French, Welsh and English peoples in a web knotted by the tirelessly reforming Cistercian Order, and, not least, by the ambitions of his own line which he inherited through the deaths of firstly his father, then his eldest brother, his cousin, and lastly his brother, Énna, who reigned for a mere nine years.

The strife which lacerated Ireland at that time was a continuing part of the evolution of the major ruling families' ambitions.

What was the moral and legal milieu into which Diarmait Mac Murchada was born? It was a society in which a major office or position was the exclusive property of one particular family by hereditary right, whether ruler, lawyer, teacher, physician or poet, and in many instances bishop or abbot. Each family in its distinctive and undiluted or exclusive position had the benefit of all the previous generations' wisdom and study in that field. The chief hereditary Uí Chennselaig lawyer, Ua Dórain, for example, as with any other major profession, could not be removed or appointed at the king's pleasure. From a very early period their persons and property were declared inviolate by law. The *ollamh*, or professor of literature and philosophy, ranked next in precedence to the monarch himself, and he received a considerable salary by any standard. Like privileges were extended to all the degrees of the legal, historical, musical and poetic professions according to rank.

The main recurring theme in the records of the Irish society of Mac Murchada is the regard for individual rights. The land of his ruling territory did not belong totally to the ruler. The ruler, elected from the hereditary ruling family, had his clearly delineated sphere of activity no less than the lawyer or veterinary surgeon. The king had the responsibility of being ruler, judge and military commander. The task of selecting the man fit to bear it evolved on the electors of the territory. Lastly, and in Mac Murchada's case of grave importance, no holder of one hereditary profession could become a representative of another hereditary profession. The judge's family could not become physicians, nor the poet's rulers.

In the Church, clerical celibacy was not obligatory but was disregarded in fact. Both the Ua Briain bishops of Killaloe, Donncha and Considine, founded families. Again, this caused no distress to anyone at home, though it did to the prelates from places where harsher concepts prevailed. Ireland had evolved its own moral and legal code different to Roman law and indifferent to certain Christian precepts. Ireland's moral and legal system was loosely codified in the tracts of the Brehon laws, laws preserved and developed from prehistoric times, handed down and developed by the hereditary lawyers called *Breitheamhain*.

Gaelic Ireland's outlook on life, even up to the seventeenth century, was unlike what it is today. 700 years after St Patrick's mission it was quite natural, normal and legal for a man to take a second wife into his home while his first wife was still there.[4] It was not an earth-shattering experience if a wife had a child for another man. There was no such thing as an 'illegitimate' child, and if a man wanted another woman but could not for some reason add her permanently to his household, he could live with her for a while. The Brehon laws took into account all these arrangements and everyone's rights were protected. The child born out of wedlock had rights. The husband of the woman who bore another man's child had his rights – the other man bore the entire cost of rearing his offspring. Above all, women had equal rights with men, which was nowhere more evident than in the law on separation by which a woman was entitled to draw from her husband's house not only what she brought in at the wedding but also the fruit of her labours.

If, for example, a man and woman married who were social and economic equals and their marriage was of their own free will, the wife was called a wife of equal rank and the consent of both was necessary to make any contract binding. A distinction was made between the first wife, known in law as the *cétmuinter*, and other wives or mistresses assumed during her occupancy of her husband's home. (Their rights and the rights of their children were scrupulously regulated by law also.) If a first wife was found insufficient and her husband introduced a second one across the threshold there were other legal obligations to be fulfilled. The second wife was also due a marriage settlement in property or valuables. However, that second wife's settlement had to be given not to her but to the first and principle wife. In addition, an honour price would have to be given to the first wife by the second wife and again by the husband involved. Furthermore, if all parties were agreeable to face the future together, another new marriage settlement was made on the first wife.

Affairs of this nature were in order in Diarmait's day. Trial marriages were normal. Unions, temporary, permanent and duplicated, were catered for in the Brehon laws. Repudiations were bilateral and common. The most frequently repeated example among the prominent is that of Gormlaith, sister of Máel Mórda, king of Leinster, who was married to, and was successively repudiated by the Norse king of Dublin, Máel Sechnaill II, high king of Ireland, and Brian Bóruma.[5] A testimony to the sagacity of the Brehon law was its recognition of mental cruelty among the seven major grounds for separation. In a nation where poems and poetry were regarded in awe, a wife had sufficient grounds for separation if her husband circulated a false story 'or satire about her until she was laughed at'.

These traditions died out slowly in Ireland. Over thirty years after the religious upheaval called the Reformation, Campion wrote:

> *Yea, even in this day, where the cleargie is fainte, they can be content to marrie for a year and a day of probation, and at the yeare's end to return her home uppon any light quarrels, if the gentlewoman's friendes bee weake and unable to avenge the injury.*[6]

The archbishop of Canterbury, Lanfranc, wrote in 1074 in identical terms to Gofraid, king of Viking Dublin, and Toirdelbach Ua Briain, the high king:

> *We hear that marriages in your kingdom are dissolved without any cause, and wives exchanged; and that blood relations under colour of marriage or otherwise do not fear to unite openly and without blame, contrary to canonical prohibition.*[7]

All violations against persons were dealt with under the Brehon law. In the case of theft or murder, the punishment was by fine according to rank and circumstances. Capital punishment for murder was not practised. Vengeance was recognised certainly as a duty, but the Brehon law's objective was to encourage the offended to eschew revenge and to submit the case to the hereditary judges for arbitration.

The most highly-prized commodity in twelfth-century Ireland was the cow. Accordingly, the cow appears with regularity in Irish literature. The penalty for first degree murder was twenty-one cows. In addition, however, there was an honour price which varied with the eminence of the slain. For example, a king's honour price was eighty-four cows in addition to the common fine. The honour price for a dairyman's murder ('the highest of the non-noble classes') was three cows. A *cumal* was the name given to the unit of value which was the equivalent of three cows.

Whatever about the wide interpretation and comprehension of the Brehon Law, the main significance is that to the Ireland of Diarmait all other philosophies were foreign.

The kingdom of Leinster formed approximately the south-east quarter of Ireland. It was the part of Ireland in full and constant communication with Britain and the mainland of Europe, because of its close proximity to both.[8] The horizons of its rulers and peoples did not begin and end in Ireland, but extended to the Norse and Mediterranean fringes of the known world. The influences and experiences gained by this communication were not shared by any other kingdom or ruler in Ireland to the same extent which may partly explain why the Leinstermen resented and resisted the central authority whether it was of the king at Tara or of Brian Bóruma in 1014. It was the Leinstermen who allied themselves with the Norse at the Battle of Clontarf.[9]

No Leinster monarch had ever established himself as undisputed king of Ireland, but the one who came closest was Diarmait's great-grandfather, Diarmait Mac Máel na mBó, who was not only the first of his family to claim and establish the title of king of Leinster and the foreigners (the Norse), but who also became the most powerful ruler in Ireland.[10] 'Diarmait Mac Máel na mBó could command Leath Mogha, Meath, Connaught and Ulster, therefore, by judgement of all he was reputed sufficient monarch of the whole.' He was proclaimed in the Annals 'king of Wales and the Isles and of Dublin and the southern half.' He fell in battle at the height of his power, in 1072, but the memory of his claim, his ambition and his accomplishment thrived in the heartland of his own family's ruling territory called Uí Chennselaig or what roughly includes modern counties Wexford, Carlow, south-west Wicklow, part of south-east Laois and an eastern slice of county Kilkenny.

The geographic positioning of county Wexford had great significance. It was a unit on its own, cut off from the rest of Ireland. Wales was a mere fifty miles away. This particular area of Mac Murchada's ruling family was bounded to the south by the Atlantic, to the west by the river Barrow and the Blackstairs mountain range, to the north by the Wicklow mountains and to the east by the Irish Sea, so that from a strategic point of view it occupied an easily defended position, a factor which remained important right up until modern times.

The county had one ferocious aspect. Its south-east corner, a low shelf of rock stabbing into the Atlantic current, is known as Carnsore Point. For several thousand years, until the advent of the Tuskar Lighthouse, it attacked vessels of all sizes with annual regularity. From this harsh corner two developments emerged. One was the fear by the inhabitants of pre-Christian times that there was an implacable demon in residence. They gathered to the low promontory and the evidence of their occupancy can be seen to this day in the harvest of raths in the area which includes the largest ringed rath in Ireland, and, almost on the point, a minor rath, the importance of which can be estimated by the presence in its centre of a later Christian oratory.[11] In AD 180 the Egyptian cartographer Ptolemy mapped Carnsore Point, from sailors' accounts, and whether to placate the spirits or acknowledge the presence of druid worship, it was given the name of Hieron Akron or Sacred Promintory. The disasters and wrecks which occurred there were a source of livelihood to the people on shore until recent times.

In the eighth century the Scandinavian sea raiders, whom we call the Norse or the Vikings, discovered Ireland. The first centuries of their visitations were barbarous. The invocation added to the prayers of the Irish beseeched 'from the fury of the Norse, O Lord deliver us.' But as time passed they became amenable to trade and military agreements with the Irish. The Norse did not occupy large tracts of land. They established a network of independent settlements or city states along the coast. In Leinster's sphere of influence at the time of Diarmait they had been established for 300 years in Dublin, Wicklow, Arklow, Wexford, Clonmines in Bannow Bay and Waterford.[12] Dublin had been developed into one of the most important trading hubs of Atlantic Europe. Its overlordship at the height of Mac Murchada dominance gave the Uí Chennselaig kings a substantial increase in power. The Norsemen had established their own coinage, cathedrals, magistrates, trade, fortified walls, bishops and, in the case of the town of Clonmines in Bannow Bay, they minted silver from the lead ore which they mined, an industry for which they were renowned.

At the time of our account Christianity had been embraced by the Norse. However, they were not satisfied with the situation in the Irish Church and so had their bishops consecrated by Canterbury. It was not that the Irish Church was any worse in its habits than some of the notorious episodes in papal history or in the sagas of sex and simony that disgraced the mediaeval Church. It was that in addition to a determined independence of Rome, there were clergy who were confused as to the message they should be preaching. For example, by established and accepted Irish norms, the see of St Patrick in Armagh was for fifteen generations filled by hereditary succession and in eight cases had been filled by married laymen.[13]

Hereditary succession also applied in some cases to the superioress of a convent where ruling families nominated the woman to be appointed. A regular hierarchy with twenty-six duly appointed diocesan bishops only replaced the loose monastic organisation after the national synod of Ráith Bressail in 1111. The excessive number of bishops prior to this was mentioned by European ecclesiastics as one of the major sins of the Irish Church. There were three in what is now county Clare. But they were necessary for the situation. None of the three rulers in that region would allow the priests in his territory to be subject to the control of the neighbouring ruler's bishop.

Viewed from outside, therefore, the Irish Church and society appeared to be in moral chaos, which was of great importance as the serious senior ecclesiastics in Rome who looked and frowned on Ireland, could, and did, make and unmake emperors.

The political organisation of Leinster and Ireland[14] included so many kingdoms that their numbers would have done credit to the German empire. All were ambitious. All either subdued lesser rulers or gave tribute to greater rulers. Ireland lacked a strong central government however; one man with the vision, courage and talent to unify the vying kings. As the twelfth century approached its third decade no one with authority to fill the throne of Ireland with clear and unqualified supremacy was apparent.

In Leinster itself Mac Murchada supremacy had been established for a comparatively short period – there were eleven free states, according to the *Book of Rights,* each with its unchanging ruling family, few of whom had not at some stage had a taste of ruling Leinster. There were also non-free states or tributary states.

These included the Norse city states and with them was numbered Osraige. The most important factor to remember is that supremacy was maintained over them by military force.

TWO

Ferns

Dawn spills across the dreary Welsh crags, crosses the waves of the Irish Sea, the meadows, the Slaney river valley and the foothills of the mountains separating the people of Diarmait Mac Murchada's ancestral homeland from their neighbours in Wicklow, Kilkenny and Waterford.

Hidden by the green camouflage in this valley is Ferns, the capital of the kings of Uí Chennselaig, now the kings of Leinster and the Norse. Enough remains of the twelfth century in Ferns today to indicate its existence over 800 years. It was once almost a backwater, seemingly contradicting it as a location of strife, horror, and the plotting of the powerful. Its mighty ruined castle, churches, abbey, towers and ancient cathedral remains are still scattered over a large enough area to summon in the imagination a picture of the mediaeval town.

Diarmait Mac Donnchada Mac Murchada was born at Ferns in the year 1110, the third son of Donnchadh Mac Murchada, the king of Leinster and the Norse.[1] His mother was Órlaith, daughter of Gille Michíl Mac Bráenáin of Uí Máel Rubae, and Uchdelb, the daughter of the king of Uí Felmeda. Their base of power was at Kilteel and their territory spread between Laraghbyrne, Maynooth and the Dublin mountains. He was never to find lasting security. The sons of kings were frequently offered in treaties to other monarchs as hostages for the good behaviour of their fathers. This did not inevitably mean uncomfortable conditions as a royal hostage was regarded as a member of his captive's family and many an unexpected dynastic alliance was secured by matrimony.[2]

There was a complication in Ireland. A king was not succeeded automatically by his eldest son. A king was elected, and while the presiding king would be a member of the ruling house the man elected could be the third son, or brother or nephew of the deceased king.[3] This meant constant competition among the ambitious in the family and it was not unknown to have six *righdamhna*, that is, six worthy of inauguration in the event of a king's death. Nevertheless these considerations would hardly put a boy like Diarmait on the alert until his later teen years.

Diarmait Mac Murchada's early years were marked by a cycle of appalling climatic conditions. When he was one year old a winter of remarkable severity with prolonged frost and snow resulted in the death of both wild and domestic animals. The immediate economic result of this was to increase the value of the cow. Four years later an even worse winter ravished Diarmait's homeland in particular. The snow and frost lasted from December to February resulting in the wholesale death of birds, cattle and people. The very next year a great famine and pestilence struck the whole of southern Ireland which spread through churches, forts and districts, causing desolation to an inconceivable degree.[4]

When Diarmait was only five years of age, his father, Donnchadh, was attacked by an alliance of Domnall Ua Briain, a direct descendant of Brian Bóruma, and the Norse of Dublin who owed Donnchadh Mac Murchada fealty.[5] In the rage of battle Diarmait's father was slain at Dublin by the Norse. Not only did Diarmait lose his father, his father's body was violated by being buried with a dog.[6] Another version states that peace had been restored, with Diarmait's father wining and dining his reconciled hosts in the great Norse Hall of Dublin when he was passed a poisoned cup. After his death he was then buried with a dog. One way or another the insult was never forgotten and partly explains the implacable hatred of the Norse that ultimately inflamed Diarmait in the closing years of his reign. To complete the woe of his family, Diarmait's eldest brother fell in battle, in 1115, while deciding the Ua Briain succession in Thomond.[7]

Diarmait was sent as a foster child to a minor king, Ua Cáellaide, who ruled a very significant portion of Osraige.[8] This created bonds of lasting affection and loyalty that nourished Diarmait all his life. The care of foster children was carefully expounded by the Brehon Law. The son of a high-ranking nobleman was to be taught swimming, shooting, horsemanship, chess playing and horn playing. 'A king's son shall have horses in times of races.' A horse was to be supplied for the child at seven years, and horsemanship taught. Payment was considerable in modern currency equivalent. For the son of the lowest order of chief it was three cows and from that it increased by degrees to the son of a king for whom the fee was from eighteen to thirty cows. Since girls were considered to be a heavier responsibility and unable to help greatly in a man's tasks the fee was higher. In cases where children were left without parents or guardians and required protection, the Brehon Law laid down that they should be placed in fosterage under suitable persons at the expense of their family.

The effects of fosterage were remarkable. Foster children were frequently more attached to their foster parents and foster brothers than to their own family. Cases occurred where 'a man has voluntarily laid down his life to save the life of his foster father or foster brother'. The system was successful enough to last until the eighteenth century in Ireland. Fosterage was considered to end at mating age which in the case of a boy was considered to be seventeen. In no one was the affection to foster parents better exemplified than in Diarmait Mac Murchada.

Diarmait's new home was not far from Ferns. The Ua Cáellaide territory was divided in two. The northern portion lay in the north of Osraige, the other lay in the south, west of modern New Ross and included modern Rosbercon with its hinterland. The strategic significance had no doubt occurred to Diarmait's father in sending his son there. So the young son of Leinster's king flowered amidst affectionate attention, unthreatened by the likelihood of becoming king unless a series of events with dire consequences materialised.

Materialise they did. The death of Diarmait's father and of his eldest available son caused the electors of Uí Chennselaig to choose a successor from another branch of the family. His name was Diarmait Mac Énna Mac Murchada.[9] The remaining sons of the dead king, Énna, Diarmait and Murchad, were, because of their youth, ineligible for election according to Brehon Law. The new king's reign was short. In 1117, the year of the great plague, he died in Dublin, having nevertheless achieved recognition as king of Leinster and the Norse.[10] Énna Mac Murchada, Diarmait's eldest surviving brother, was now elected to succeed.[11] Énna Mac Murchada had matured in the two years of his cousin Diarmait Mac Énna's reign and he was a success from the start. Though young he was quite adept at walking the political tight-rope and made his own imprint on Uí Chennselaig policies and alliances. He made friends and enemies as it suited his purpose and this saw him on occasions both a staunch ally and a beneficiary of the high king Toirdelbach Ua Conchobair, as well as a partner in a confederation plotting Ua Conchobair's downfall.[12] In retrospect, the most contrary aspect of his reign was his alliance with Tigernán Ua Ruairc of Bréifne, who was to become his brother Diarmait's fierce enemy. By 1125 he was unchallenged and acknowledged as king of Leinster and the Norse by Toirdelbach Ua Conchobair. In 1126 his unexpected death in the Norse town of Wexford thrust Uí Chennselaig into disarray.[13] Diarmait Mac Murchada was sixteen years of age when the news was related to him that Énna, his brother the king, had died, not in battle nor by the assassin's knife. The news was alarming both for his foster parents and the office holders of the Mac Murchada hegemony in Ferns.

There were few choices now left open to the electors of Uí Chennselaig. Firstly, a ruler of Uí Chennselaig would have to personally stake his claim to the kingship of Leinster, for which prize there were at least three other aspirants. And who had the electors left to choose from? From the dead king's family there were only Diarmait, sixteen, Murchad, his younger brother and perhaps a cousin. There was no loophole in the Brehon Law. No one who was not of age could be elected. The ritual at an election is laid down in the Brehon code.[14] Each freeman of the rank of aire, or chieftain, in the Mac Murchada home ruling area, had a vote. A conference was held to which all the electors proceeded with full retinue and there they remained for approximately three days if there were several candidates. At the end of this period the elected man's name was announced.

The name which emerged from this forum was Diarmait Mac Donnchada Mac Murchada. As he was then only sixteen, it was an election which set aside the precept of the Brehon Law and that must have been an outrage to many. It was so much in opposition to the known rule that a later historian, Ó Cléirigh, was to find the entry indicating the age of Diarmait Mac Murchada in the *Book of Leinster* unacceptable. The transition of power this time required a calculated conspiracy of the electors amongst whom were numbered the chief lawyer Ua Dórain and the new bishop of Ferns, Ua Cattáin. The conspirators had decided to gamble. They had overcome any contrary claims, and the legitimisation of their assembly's choice awaited only the inauguration ceremonies through which power would be properly transferred.

The inauguration stone of the Mac Murchada kings of the Uí Chennselaig, as for their predecessors for centuries, was at Loggan Lower in the north-west corner of the modern county Wexford border with county Wicklow. Its old title was Leac Mic Eochadha, or in English, Kehoe's flagstone. This flagstone was situated in a superb, elevated and ancient Bronze Age burial complex. Mac Eochadha, the head of his bardic family, held the inherited privilege of inaugurating the successive kings of Uí Chennselaig. The site complex, enclosed by a fosse, contained cyst and urn burials in what was a royal rath. It indicated both continuity with remote tradition and the royal patriarchs of a bygone age, and it had heroic visual properties as well, crowned by the benign hill close by, still known as Croaghan Kinsella. The land to the south of the inauguration site formed the core, hub and heartland of Uí Chennselaig. It has some of the richest, most easily worked, free draining and productive soils in Europe for grain, grass or timber and streams and rivers, notably the Slaney, rippling with salmon. Throughout the ages it possessed the source of wealth and power.

The inauguration place, which was granted sacred status

afforded visibility for a widespread audience. The man taking the dominant role would be visible from practically all points across the valley and mountain foothills, particularly at the most vital part of the ceremony when he stood by the inauguration stone itself. Diarmait Mac Murchada was the focus of attention like any newly elected king before him. According to long prescribed ritual, the rulers of the smaller kingdoms of Uí Chennselaig stood with their retinues in preordained places. The office holders, lawyers and administrators of the Mac Murchada government were there, as were the poets and historians, to record and witness the vital moment of legal continuity. Bishops, abbots and other leading ecclesiastics were also present, all of them sharing an anxiety for a smooth transition of power.

Mac Muirgeasa, the ollamh of Ferns, intoned the laws which were to bind the candidate in service to and in defence of his people. That concluded, Diarmait Mac Murchada took the oath to observe the laws which regulated his conduct, to uphold the historic traditions of his kingdom and to govern his people with strict justice.

Diarmait Mac Donnchada Mac Murchada was then approached by another hereditary office-holder who held the authority to bestow power, Mac Eochadha. Mac Eochadha handed Diarmait a straight, white, slender rod. It was the emblem of his authority and was symbolic of what his reign should ensure in legal decisions and behaviour: a high standard of conduct and strict impartiality. At that moment power was legally passed on to Diarmait Mac Murchada. The new king put his sword to one side and, holding the rod in one hand, he turned three times from left to right. He then turned three times from right to left in honour of the Blessed Trinity and to take in with his eyes the land of his kingdom from all directions. Mac Eochadha then loudly shouted Diarmait's name, 'Mac Donnchada Mac Murchada.' Then ruler after ruler, prelate after prelate, dignitary after dignitary, according to rank, echoed the shout and it was taken up by the concourse of people. Thus began one of the most momentous reigns in Ireland's history.

Diarmait became intimately familiar with his native coast and aware, moreover, of the political systems, trends and evolutions sweeping Europe, for in his kingdom the stories, names of streets, squares and entertainments of ports like Bristol or Constantinople were household topics. Of the overseas cities with which he became familiar, Bristol was the most important, even though St David's was little more than fifty miles away and Pembroke a short distance more. Bristol was the great place of trade for Diarmait and all seafarers, Norse and Irish, in his kingdom. It was the marketplace where the knowledge and gossip of the known world were swapped at first hand and, most significant of all, it was the city with whose rulers Diarmait continued close relations.

So besides his own culture there were other cultures in which he grew up and which he observed and compared at close quarters. These included the Viking, the Norman, the Welsh and the English languages and systems of trade. The progress of the Norse in his own kingdom was remarkable. For it was they who, as busy as soldier ants, explored every creek and inlet exhaustively. Near Clonmines, at the top of what proved to be one of the most important water inlets in Ireland, Bannow Bay, the Norse had discovered the presence of lead ore from which they minted silver. Its worth was well known in Diarmait's time and the mines were still in operation over 400 years later. As for the Norse in his own region at Wexford, there had been decades of trade, intercourse and occasionally warfare in the coexistence of Gael and Gall. The Vikings in Wexford had their churches, regular parishes and warrior saints like St Michael the Archangel, while outside the gates of the Norse town were the Irish churches for travellers and traders, like St Brigid's. The Irish market and township to the north of the Norse walls continued as a market place into modern times with fruit, apples, fish, cabbage seedlings and butter still occasionally on public display.

THREE

Power

The kingship of all Ireland had not been held by a widely accepted monarch for some time. For the ten years prior to Diarmait's election, the king of Connaught, Toirdelbach Mór Ua Conchobair, had been battling towards the high kingship[1]. It was his life's ambition to make Connaught first among equals and superior by force of arms. The method he used was the classic of divide and dominate. He made war from Connaught and imposed his will on almost all other kingships in Ireland. Military victory was followed by the divisions of kingdoms, with reliables getting one half. The making and unmaking of other kings and taking hostages were common practice. Early in his career, in 1115, Toirdelbach divided Meath between two members of the Ua Máel Sechlainn ruling family, one of whom promptly killed the other. It was Munster's turn in 1118 when for the first time since 1014 a descendant of Brian Bóruma was forced to share his kingdom with a Mac Carthaig, and to demonstrate that he would tolerate no nonsense, Toirdelbach hurled the ancestral Ua Briain stronghold, stones and timber, into the river Shannon at Kincora.

Toirdelbach then focused his interest on the surviving Ua Máel Sechlainn brother of Meath. In 1120 Ua Máel Sechlainn was expelled from his kingdom. The then elderly Uí Néill claimant to the high kingship, Domnall Mac Lochlainn of the north, began to regard this Toirdelbach Ua Conchobair as a serious threat. Mac Lochlainn decided it was time to curb Ua Conchobair and went to the defence of the deposed ruler of Meath. Here another normal Irish gambit was exemplified, for Ua Conchobair made what has been written down as the 'false peace'. And Ua Máel Sechlainn was restored. Ua Conchobair now harassed Ua Máel Sechlainn. For many years he was to return to buffet him, expel him and extract

hostages. The survival of Ua Máel Sechlainn is one of the endurance sagas of Ireland. But whatever of that, it was Diarmait Mac
Murchada's sympathy with the ruler of Meath and his antipathy
to Ua Conchobair which were to have momentous significance for
Ireland.

In 1125, the last year of Diarmait's boyhood, Ua Conchobair
once more expelled Leinster's northern neighbour, Ua Máel Sechlainn of Meath. Ua Conchobair placed four rulers over Meath.
One of them was dispatched at an early stage – and that left three.
One of these three demands serious attention for his reputation
as one of the most abrasive figures in Irish history, a man whose
talent was for inflicting suffering. His name was Tigernán Ua
Ruairc, ruler of Bréifne.

The campaigns of Ua Conchobair at the time of the 'false peace'
indicate the modest length of time a ruler, politician or soldier
could slumber. Prior to his Meath expeditions, Ua Conchobair
built several bridges across the Shannon at Athlone for transport-
ing troops and to ease conquest. They were no sooner built than
destroyed by hands governed by fear. In 1121 he moved south to
one of the most fertile and productive areas of Ireland, Munster.
Here he laid waste to Desmond 'from Mag Femin to Tralee, both
lands and churches, namely, seventy churches or a little more, until
he caused the people of Munster to cry aloud.' In the same year he
made another sweep into Munster as far as Lismore and 'obtained
innumerable cattle as booty.'

His next expedition into Munster took place in 1122 and 1123.
The people of Munster yielded. They gave hostages to Ua Conchobair, the highest ranking of whom was the king of Desmond's
son. Ua Conchobair killed them within a year when there was a
general uprising against him. Énna Mac Murchada, Diarmait's
immediate predecessor was among Ua Conchobair's enemies in
this uprising but by 1125 friendly relations had been restored and
Énna Mac Murchada's kingship of Norse Dublin and Leinster
was consolidated.

This, then was the climate of power which existed before Diarmait's election. It was one of potential stability with Ua Conchobair predominant in Ireland and the allied force of Énna Mac Murchada secure in Leinster and Dublin. The power vacuum created by the unexpected death of Énna in Wexford early in 1126 precipitated the total alienation between the young Diarmait Mac Murchada and Ireland's strongest king, Toirdelbach Ua Conchobair.

It took Ua Conchobair a short time to assess the qualities of the ruler elected to succeed Énna Mac Murchada. When he did react, Ua Conchobair created a storm of war. His actions were recorded in the annals. He intended to 'constitute a king' and Diarmait was thrown out of the way. He was lucky not to have been mutilated or killed.

Ua Conchobair mobilised one of the great crusades of his life. Leinster, with support from the Norse of Dublin, Wicklow, Arklow and Wexford, was a massive opponent to overcome. The first thing he did was to issue a declaration that his own son, Conchobar Ua Conchobair, was henceforth king of Leinster and Dublin. He next established a huge military base in Ormonde which lay a few miles to the west of the Barrow river boundary to the south of Diarmait's kingdom. From 1 August 1126 and into the following year, he set out on punitive expeditions on land as well as by sea, employing 190 ships. The chronicles record the great numbers of cattle and prisoners taken. Munster revolted. Leinster mounted what defence it could. Every one of the newly surrendered Munster and Leinster hostages in Ua Conchobair's hands was put to death.

The king who was forced upon Dublin and Leinster, Ua Conchobair's son, was deposed. However, Ua Conchobair was not going to allow the Mac Murchada interests to predominate. The high king decided that firm action would instil subservience in Diarmait Mac Murchada, his supporters and people. Ua Conchobair accepted the deposition of his son, but ingeniously chose to replace him with a member of a family which had provided many Leinster kings, a family subjugated by the Mac Murchadas on their own drive to power. His name was Domnall Mac Fáeláin. He therefore installed a man whom no one in Leinster could describe as a 'stranger'. He was a man who, it was hoped, would not only be ultimately accepted by the north Leinstermen and the Norse, but would also be a reliable pro-Ua Conchobair militant in the kingdom.

Mac Murchada reacted with outrage. Ua Conchobair invaded Leinster in response. The campaign against Leinster took place in 1128 when Diarmait was eighteen. It was a hot year of drought. Ua Conchobair did not take a prominent part in this expedition himself but his commander was a man of insatiable violence. His name was Tigernán Ua Ruairc, king of Bréifne. He administered the greatest lesson to Diarmait, a lesson which fuelled the hatred that almost lost Ireland to the Gael.[2] Ua Ruairc's repeated violence was born of frustration. His father had been king of Bréifne and king of Connaught as well. When Toirdelbach Ua Conchobair seized overall power in Connaught Tigernán Ua Ruairc was reduced to the margins and compelled to accept a subordinate position.

In 1128 the expedition to subdue and humiliate Mac Murchada set out. That it succeeded cannot be denied. The expedition pierced through Leinster as far as Wexford, wheeled around the outskirts of the kingdom and thence back to Dublin. Ua Ruairc lost no opportunity to undermine Diarmait Mac Murchada or to feed the hatred which instigated forty years of revenges and counter-revenges. He aimed to make Mac Murchada an economic as well as a military cripple. There was wholesale destruction of cows along the route of the expedition, in addition to burning. The result was total humiliation for the young Mac Murchada. The mistake its leaders made was to underestimate Diarmait Mac Murchada, probably because of his youth. If they had not, there is no doubt that he would have been killed or blinded.

Mac Murchada's power was devastated but not completely crushed. No formal submission was made to Ua Conchobair but no rash claims to the northern half of Leinster presided over by Mac Fáeláin were uttered. The time had come to lick wounds and survey of the prevailing circumstances. Diarmait consulted the shrewd minds of his electors and advisers.

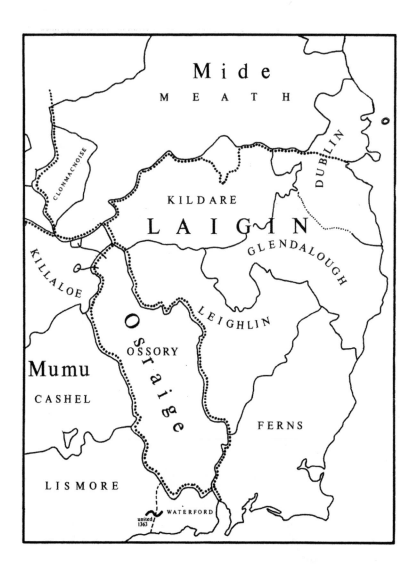

The diocesan boundaries created by the Synod of Raith Bressail in 1111 corresponded to the major political boundaries. Mac Murchada's Uí Chennselaig at its greatest twelfth century expansion is identified in the boundaries of the diocese of Ferns and Leighlin.

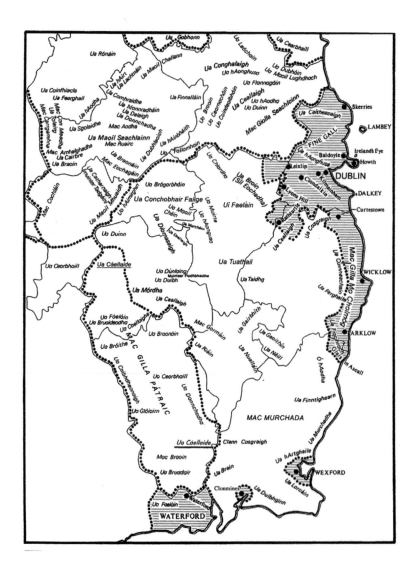

Ruling families in the areas in which the Mac Murchadas were most politically active.

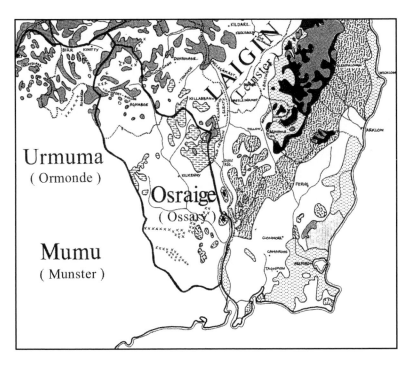

SOILS AND POPULATION

- BOG
- GRANITE
- ACIDIC
- POOR DRAINAGE
- MILLSTONE GRITS & SHALE *v. poor soil*
- EXCESSIVE DRAINAGE
- SANDSTONE
- LARGE LIME ENRICHMENT *fertile, arable & pasture*

BOUNDARIES OF
MAJOR KINGDOMS

When the first soil type maps were published by An Foras Taluntais (Lee and Haughton, 1968), it was found that the political boundaries in Uí Chennselaig were, approximately, the same as the soil type boundaries. The strong ruling families were found on the most fertile, easily worked soils. The families who in time had been marginalised were pushed to poorer and the poorest soils. Mac Murchada and Síol Mac Brain (Ua Brain) were situated on superb soils. Ua Duibhginn in Uí Bairraiche (Bargy) were herded to the worst following their earlier centuries of power. *(Reproduced by kind permission of Teagasc)*

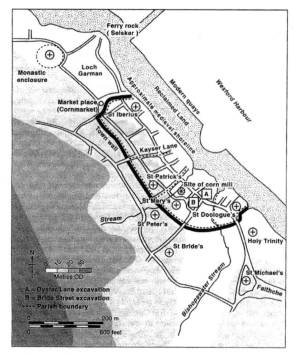

Twelfth century Norse Wexford with surrounding wall. Gaelic Loch Garman, where defensive arrangements were deemed unnecessary, had developed around the Slaney River ferry crossing from remote times. *(Reproduced by kind permission of Wexford Historical Society)*

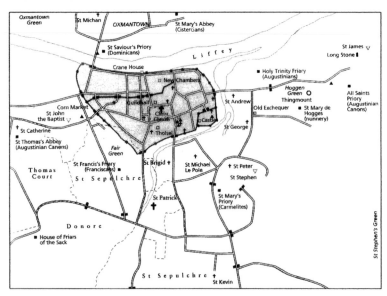

Norse Dublin in the reign of Diarmait Mac Murchada.
(Reproduced by kind permission of Jonathan Bardon and Stephen Conlin, from their book, Dublin, One Thousand Years of Wood Quay*)*

An early Christian cross on the perimeter of the cathedral grounds in Ferns, Co. Wexford. *(Photograph by Hemingway and Doyle)*

The remnants of the Augustinian abbey founded by Diarmait Mac Murchada in Ferns, Co. Wexford in 1158. *(Photograph by Hemingway and Doyle)*

The remnants of Ferns Castle show different stages of development and stone-work. Built on the existing Mac Murchada castle its early thirteenth century development is credited to Diarmait Mac Murchada's granddaughter, Isabella, and her husband, William Marshall. *(Photograph by James B. Curtis)*

Baltinglass Abbey, Co. Wicklow, founded in 1148. *(Reproduced by kind permission of the Department of the Environment, Heritage and Local Government)*

The campanile in Trinity College Dublin, site of the monastery founded by Diarmait Mac Murchada for the canons regular of the Augustinians in 1166. His brother-in-law, Lorcán Ó Tuathail, had been consecrated first Irish archbishop of Norse Dublin in 1162. *(Photograph by Patrick J. Jordan)*

The Nuns Chapel in Clonmacnoise, founded by Derbforgaill, wife of Tigernan Ua Ruairc, King of Breifne. It was completed in 1167. *(Photograph by Patrick J. Jordan)*

The broken high cross over the grave of Diarmait Mac Murchada and his son, Domnall Caomanac Mac Murchada, in the church-yard of Ferns Cathedral. *(Photograph by Hemingway and Doyle)*

Here lies the remains of
DIARMAID MAC MURCADA
(Dermot Mac Morrough)
King of Leinster
Born 1110 – Died 1171
And
Domnall Caomanac
(Son of Diarmaid)
1128 – 1175

Modern memorial at the graveside of Diarmait Mac Murchada and his son, Domnall Caomanac Mac Murchada. *(Photograph by Hemingway and Doyle)*

FOUR

The Man

Diarmait was now battened down in Uí Chennselaig, and appeared to be a minor and fragile chieftain. Diarmait and his advisers knew that every day might be their last as they were under threat from rivals and neighbouring kings, Irish or Norse. Any weakened dynasty was open for demolition. For a defence against annihilation Uí Chennselaig could hire Vikings, Welshmen or Bristol men, but who would be in charge but a youth of eighteen?

Diarmait Mac Murchada was left to mature in peace. The three years which followed saw him gather strength. A period of consolidation was essential. It was a time for amity with the Norse, for there was no more fickle neighbour. The Norse depended on their wits for survival because they could easily have been overwhelmed. Accordingly, they allied themselves to the man they had sufficient reason to believe would be the ultimate winner. Diarmait's task was to establish himself as that leader, and this was of paramount value not only for trade and shipping but also from a military point of view. He would ignore the man nominated by Ua Conchobair as king of Leinster and Dublin but the Norsemen did not ignore him: 'they sent him away,' thereby withdrawing recognition.

It appeared that he was doomed for nothing more exalted than the position of a minor chieftain in his family's core ruling area with a life of oppression and raids before him. In the meantime the fact that no opportunity presented itself for expansion of his lands was a blessing, for it gave him a few years to live his youth. The apprenticeship yielded one addition which was to have long significance in Ireland and outside it. Diarmait fathered a son, Domnall, who was placed in fosterage and was therefore given the additional definition Domnall Cáemánach Mac Murchada. He was to be the progenitor of the line known in modern times as Mac Murrough

Kavanagh. Nothing was recorded of his mother.

Apart from romantic interludes, those years of Mac Murchada's life must have been spent in planning, training and education. The man who reappeared at the end of that period was a wiser, more cautious man. From that time on, Diarmait Mac Murchada moved only if the wind was at his back.

The enormous harvests in 1130 of every kind of agricultural produce helped strengthen Mac Murchada's position.[1] This unprecedented increase in wealth strengthened morale, and, in the absence of military activity there was time to contemplate the prosperity. There was one other development during this period: Tigernán Ua Ruairc of Bréifne, the devastator of Uí Chennselaig, added to his reputation by defeating and killing the king of Meath, Diarmait Ua Máel Sechlainn.

In 1131, three years after his humiliation by Ua Ruairc, fortune smiled on Mac Murchada. There was a simultaneous revolt against the high king[2] from all sides. Forces from Meath, Munster and from the Uí Néill king of Ulster raged against him. Suddenly the high king found himself reaping vengeance. He was unbowed, unrepentant, but in deep trouble. It was in these propitious circumstances that the germ of Mac Murchada ambition was reactivated not merely in Diarmait himself but in the chief men of Uí Chennselaig. With renewed prosperity came ambition for advancement.

Matrimony has created solutions in many political and dynastic situations. The arranged marriage in different societies can prove either disasterous or congenial and satisfactory. There are no sagas or myths surrounding Diarmait Mac Murchada's first marriage. In or around this period he married Sadb[3]. She was the daughter of the king of Uí Fáeláin, Cerball Mac Fáeláin, the descendant of many kings of Leinster whose core ruling territory was in what roughly corresponds to north Kildare today.[4] Whatever the arrangements for the prescribed union were, it can be taken that mutual benefit was one of the major considerations.

The first major military venture by Mac Murchada may seem shocking to us today. A confluence of remarkable circumstances presented itself, prominent amongst which was a bloody dispute between north Leinster's royal families and the succession of the abbacy of Kildare. The powers of the abbey of Kildare were not merely religious but political as well and have no comparable counterpart in modern times. The abbey was a double monastery with nuns under an abbess and monks under an abbot occupying separate residential buildings. The great church was common to both sexes but screens allowed for no visual contact. St Brigid had ruled over both nuns and monks and this primacy of a woman, an abbess, continued in the centuries of the monastery's expansion after her death. The line of abbesses of Kildare are recorded down to the late twelfth century under that title of singular prestige, Comharba Brighde, the successor and inheritor of Brigid.

For generations the office of abbess of Kildare was in the giving of the king of Leinster. Diarmait's aunt, Gormlaith, had been abbess of Kildare in a period of Mac Murchada dominance. In 1127 when Mac Murchada power was inconsequential, the Uí Failge claimants to Leinster succeeded in having their nominee, their ruler's daughter, Mór, installed as abbess of Kildare. Mór had displaced the daughter of Cerball Mac Fáeláin, king of Uí Fáeláin, the sister of the temporarily nominated king of Dublin. A ruling family was scorned, a daughter humiliated. Battle between the two dynasties was inevitable.[5] It was not a minor battle between mere foot soldiers in a monastic town but a struggle of such vehemence that the king of Uí Fáeláin, Cerball Mac Fáeláin, was himself killed, leading his men into battle and defeat in the centre of Kildare.

By 1132 the prospect was viewed by Diarmait Mac Murchada from a different perspective. He was now married to Sadb, the daughter of the slain Uí Fáeláin king. The abbess intruded by the killers of his father-in-law was by now consolidated in the rights and jurisdiction of the abbey of Kildare. That monastic town and power base was of such significance that its control was an essential prerequisite for anyone who aspired to the kingship of Leinster. Though the entire episode might bring groans from churchmen it was not an issue of a minor or absurd nature. Diarmait Mac

Murchada decided that he would no longer be regarded as minor or absurd.

He dispatched his available forces against the monastic town and abbey of Kildare.[6] The town was stormed and 107 of the defenders were killed. The abbey itself was next. It was entered and profaned. The Ua Failge abbess, Mór, was sought and identified. She was raped.[7] Ineligible then for her high office, she was discarded. Installed in her stead to a position of power was Diarmait's cousin, also named Sadb, daughter of Glúniairn Mac Murchada. She remained securely in that role for the rest of her life and indeed for the rest of Diarmait Mac Murchada's life as well.[8]

Mac Murchada now considered the direction of his next assault on power. Two thorns in his flank remained. They were the kingdom of Osraige and the Norse city of Waterford.

Mac Murchada busied himself forging alliances with neighbouring territories, notably that of the Ua Tuathail who once were monarchs of Leinster. His pressure was effective, but despite his success he walked into the second serious miscalculation of his reign. At the age of twenty-four he led an expedition of Leinstermen into Osraige.[9] His idea that Osraige was ripe for subjection was shattered. The Osraige men resisted and wiped the ground with his men. In the slaughter that followed, Ugaire Ua Tuathail, son of the ruler of Uí Muiredaig and Uí Máil, a young man regarded to be of ruling potential by his family, lost his life. So did many others. Mac Murchada had suffered another humiliation, and Mac Gilla Pátraic, the ruler of Osraige, with newly surrendered hostages, rejoiced in triumph.

To add to Mac Murchada's woes, economic troubles spread. In 1133 and 1134 murrain, a serious blood infection spread among cows causing them to die.[10] However, Mac Murchada began to engage himself even more determinedly in winning allies. A major long-term objective was supremacy over the southern half of Ireland, or, failing that, establishing favourable alliances. The port of Waterford, the Viking cornerstone of Munster, would have to be made safe for Mac Murchada. Mac Murchada and his closest advisers made for Norse Dublin and a conference with its rulers. What transpired between the hardy Norse and Diarmait is not known, but the result was clear. The forces and skills of Dublin were put at his disposal, even to the execution of an attack on Viking Waterford itself. So a couple of months after Diarmait's defeat by Osraige, the Osraige ruler, Mac Gilla Pátraic, found an army of Norse and Uí Chennselaig men sweeping through his lands in enthusiastic retaliation. They did not stop there but swept on deep into Munster to inflict a similiar defeat on the king of Thomond, Conchobar Ua Briain. They then turned and hurled their strength on an astonished Waterford.[11]

Waterford's sentinels viewed with alarm a horde of Irish warriors, armoured and equipped before their walls. Beside them stood their brother Vikings in the armour developed over three centuries of terror from the Baltic to the Atlantic.

Surprise, slaughter and subjection followed. Guarantees and hostages for good behaviour were bestowed on the victor, and a promise of future alliance urged firmly from Conchobar Ua Briain, king of Thomond. Diarmait Mac Murchada had shown his teeth and established himself for the first time by arms as king of Leinster and the Norse, and now as overlord of the homeland of Brian Bóruma, Munster's Thomond. It was a remarkable campaign, and evidence of a resurgent Mac Murchada.

FIVE

A Force to be Reckoned With

With the high king cornered Mac Murchada established himself by degrees. In the next few years his situation altered.[1] From having to seek allies and placate antagonists he had advanced to the state of being sought after. It was no disadvantage that the high king suffered a long illness.[2] But the fortress of Waterford for the second time refused to 'enter into [Diarmait's] house' permanently.

One reason behind the Waterford men's renewed contempt for Diarmait is easily understood. They held an impregnable city, open to the sea and rivers, of which the Vikings were masters, and if they did happen to be isolated on the land side, their sea trade route was in no danger from the Irish of Leinster.

The Irish had no reputation for siege warfare. Of unquestionable courage in the open field, they regarded a city starved to death as much less painful than a wall-scaling operation. Head-on storming of fortified walls was, therefore, regarded as a form of madness. This was particularly true of Waterford whose walls encompassed a triangular enclosure with three mighty towers on each corner. Reginald's tower stands today, after 1,000 years of strife, on the water's edge. The idea of its overthrow in 1137 was not to be considered. But it was considered, for the man who wanted Waterford was no inland soldier whose horizon was bounded by the hills and woods of the midlands. Mac Murchada decided on the unexpected route, the unfamiliar route, the perilous Atlantic sea route around Carnsore Point. He had the ships, he had the men, for he had the sea-faring Norse of Dublin and Wexford on his side.

He called on the alliance entered into by Conchobar Ua Briain of Thomond, his defeated adversary of three years previously, to lay siege to Waterford on the land side.[3] Two hundred ships from Dublin and Wexford, bearing Mac Murchada's hardened men of two races, rounded Hook Head and sped up the river until they arrived rolling before the open quayside of Waterford.[4] To the citizens of Waterford it was an unforgettable sight. It forced the city's magistrates to come to the conclusion that another submission was more advantageous than a defiant last stand in the streets. Hostages and renewed guarantees left their hands for Ferns.

Another part of Munster, Desmond – which was transferred from the Ua Briain's grasp and regranted to the ruling Mac Carthaig family by the high king Ua Conchobair – was a substantial enclave in southern Ireland outside of Mac Murchada's sphere of interest. Mac Carthaig was still a protégé of the high king Ua Conchobair and though a blood bath was not to be countenanced some form of attack was worth a risk in a time of the high king's military infirmity. Mac Murchada now secured by swift mobility the submission of Mac Carthaig, king of Desmond, along with hostages.

The most valuable development, however, was not that the southern half of Ireland had 'entered his house', for one thing which experience of Irish politics taught was the brevity of 'perpetual guarantees'. The most significant development was that his ally and former adversary, Conchobar Ua Briain, who bore the greatest name in recent Irish history, that of the house of Brian Bóruma, submitted to Diarmait as overlord. Diarmait guaranteed him, in turn, the obedience of the Mac Carthaigs, though Diarmait left the implementation of securing this obedience to the Ua Briains themselves.[5] In two years the Mac Carthaig ruling family had been deposed by the Ua Briains and were compelled to take sanctuary outside their homeland to wait for a better day.

The king of Leinster now turned his attention further northwards. It would be naïve to disregard his hatred for the instrument of his first humiliation, the ruler of Bréifne, Tigernán Ua Ruairc. In 1137 Diarmait cemented his relationship with a family whose association with him was to become one of the most dramatic in Irish history and certainly the best known in English and Irish literature. He made a treaty with the king of

Meath on the north of Leinster's borders, a kingdom of the most fertile soil, production and strategic significance.[6] The name of its king was Murchad Ua Máel Sechlainn, and his kingdom formed a barrier to the ambition and turbulence of Tigernán Ua Ruairc. The king's daughter, Derbforgaill, was destined to be Tigernán Ua Ruairc's wife and Diarmait Mac Murchada's mistress. She was to inspire poems, dramas and legends, to repent, to endow and die in a convent at an advanced age with the old order she knew as a child on its way to history's archives. However that was over a generation away in 1137.

Diarmait's agreement with the ruler of Meath was a treaty of promise and fidelity. It had mutual advantages, all the greater because the two parties knew and held each other in esteem. Diarmait's esteem for Ua Máel Sechlainn was born in the days when he saw the house of Ua Máel Sechlainn made the constant victim of the high king Ua Conchobair and his bitter cohort Ua Ruairc, both of whose teeth he had felt himself. He also knew that Meath was the buffer state between Leinster and the determined expansion of Ua Ruairc and Connaught.

The treaty was very like a twentieth-century treaty defining mutual support and spheres of influence. Diarmait gave an undertaking to assist the king of Meath with his forces and at his own cost 'against anyone with as great an army,' provided that the king of Meath would allow him to enjoy without disturbance the kingdom of his wife's family, Uí Fáeláin, and also the kingdom of Uí Failge, whose rulers' ambitions he had ruptured in the over-running of Kildare. These two kingdoms had been subjected to raids from Meath. The raids were to end, and Mac Murchada was given a free hand with both territories.

Mac Murchada was never to enjoy the permanent submission of the north Leinster states. He had to be constantly alert to their manoeuvres. The four north Lenister territories upon which he must maintain a grip, if he was determined to be predominant in Leinster, were Uí Failge, Uí Fáeláin, Uí Donnchada of Cualu and Uí Muiredaig. The ruling family of Uí Donnchada of Cualu,

Mac Gilla Mo Cholmóc, administered the east coast from the very boundary of Uí Chennselaig to the gates of Viking Dublin itself. Uí Muiredaig with Uí Máil were ruled by Ua Tuathail dynasty. Throughout his long ruling life Mac Murchada was engaged with one, two, or all of them. The perpetual play and counter-play of politics in Leinster was ever present as the background to his life. It is in this context, therefore, that the significance of the Uí Chennselaig Meath treaty of 1137 must be seen. It is certain that this treaty was negotiated in the teeth of interference once more from the high king Ua Conchobair and Ua Ruairc.

The following year, in 1138, an astounding event in Irish politics took place.[7] The king of Meath, as feared, called upon Diarmait to fulfil his treaty obligation. The usual forces bearing down on Meath's lush land, as they had with monotonous repetition, were those of the high king Toirdelbach Ua Conchobair, Tigernán Ua Ruairc of Bréifne and the ruler of the northern territory of Airgialla, Donnchad Ua Cerbaill. In the words of the recorder, 'they mustered their forces to contest his own lands with Ua Máel Sechlainn'.

By horse and foot, Irish and Norse, Diarmait powered his army northwards to Meath, not knowing whether he was to be decimated by the powerful Ua Conchobair's confederacy. The two armies closed in on one another, the approximate battlefield was gauged, and the soldiers encamped. Diarmait Mac Murchada and Ua Máel Sechlainn had their plan of battle, yet as novices in major battle they flinched before the attack which must inevitably come from Connaught. They watched tensely for one week. And then came the unexpected. The high king withdrew, and Diarmait withdrew, without a crash of blade on blade, nor even the thud of a hurled rock or an exchange of a single hostage. The significance of this was not lost on participants nor beholders. The ebb of Toirdelbach Ua Conchobair's tide was in decline and Mac Murchada had watched his departure. It encouraged his belief, at twenty-eight, that the overlordship of Ireland was not outside the reach of another Leinster and Uí Chennselaig king.

There is further evidence of Mac Murchada's growing influence. In the remote north the bishop of Clogher died. His diocese corresponded with the kingdom of Airgialla ruled by Ua Cerbaill. Its ecclesiastical extent fluctuated but in the mid 1100s it covered a very wide band from Lough Derg in county Donegal to Drogheda in county Louth. Today it includes county Monaghan, most of county Fermanagh with portions of Tyrone, Cavan and Louth. The late bishop of Clogher was a brother of the dynamic reformer, Malachy.

When in 1139 the new bishop of Clogher's name was made known it was found that he was not from the north, nor from the kingdom of Airgialla. He was none other than Diarmait Mac Murchada's own foster brother, Aed Ua Cáellaide.[8] And Aed Ua Cáellaide had the recorded privilege of being Diarmait Mac Murchada's confessor.

SIX

All Leinster Far Under Hand

It took a conspiracy of fatal intent to shake Mac Murchada to alert. In 1140 a coup was successfully staged against one of the seemingly unassailable rulers in the land. To Mac Murchada's satisfaction, his mortal enemy, Tigernán Ua Ruairc of Bréifne, was deposed by his own people. Mac Murchada's cheer was dampened by anxieties of his own. The banishment of Ua Ruairc taught him some harsh realities. From 1140 to 1141 the opposition to Mac Murchada from the rulers of the north Leinster states gathered strength. Diarmait Mac Murchada was faced with the prospect of the well-knit structure of Norse and Irish in his kingdom being demolished and he himself eliminated.

The conspirators against Mac Murchada made an alarming team of confederates.

Amongst its protagonists were his wife's brother, Mac Fáeláin, Murchad Ua Tuathail and Muirchertach Mac Gilla Mo Cholmóc, son of the king of Cualu (into whose family a daughter of Diarmait's was later to marry).[1] These three dynastic representatives were not operating on their own. They were joined in conspiracy by several others. However, there were no Norsemen involved since they never involved themselves with any project unless its proponents were in a strong position and the reward evident.

Diarmait's brother-in-law, Mac Fáeláin, more than anyone else, would have to be rendered powerless and with him anyone remaining with the pretensions or capability of ruling. The threat was directed against the Mac Murchada dynasty and that dynasty reacted as one undivided unit under threat. The elimination of his brother-in-law took place when in one swift operation the entire leadership of Mac Murchada's enemies were cut down on Diarmait's orders. The man who executed the command was his brother, Murchad Mac Murchada.[2] Mac Fáeláin, Ua Tuathail, Mac Gilla Mo Cholmóc, amongst a total of seventeen, were killed or blinded. 'Thus,' as one writer puts it, 'did Diarmait like many of his compeers, secure his throne with the corpses and pierced eyeballs of his rivals.'

The practice of mutilation was invited by Brehon Law which stipulated that a king must be completely sound in body and limb. Yet the practice of blinding had come to western Europe from the east and at the time of William the Conqueror it was as common in England as it later became in Ireland. In 1136 the high king Ua Conchobair blinded his own son,[3] whom he considered a threat to himself, a deed incomprehensible to us today. Henry II, in his bogged-down campaign in Wales, blinded the sons of the Welsh princes he held as prisoners, and paraded them stumbling.[4] In later years the son of Ua Conchobair who had survived with his eyesight to claim the high kingship after the death of Toirdelbach was named Ruaidrí. On his accession he lodged his three brothers in prison and blinded the most accomplished of the three.

The result of Mac Murchada's fierce initiative is recorded, in a rather understated manner, by a contemporary writer: 'The deed brought all Leinster far under hand.' It also obliterated any notion that Mac Murchada was without steel. His ruthless deed brought Leinster under hand for a quarter of a century. Mac Murchada had solved grave problems. So had his northern adversary, Ua Ruairc. The deposed ruler of Bréifne had turned the tables on his enemies and was once more at the helm at home. This return to power by Ua Ruairc was to have consequences for Diarmait Mac Murchada in the long term.

Mac Murchada was served well by his administrators and friends, the closest of whom were men of outstanding ability. The reputations of at least two of his distinguished collaborators survive to this day. The first and most influential was Maurice Ó Regan, his councillor, secretary of state and interpreter. He was to be found always in support either at Diarmait's side or on negotiation missions, observing, recording, suggesting, urging. The second was Áed Mac Crimthainn, abbot of Terryglass, referred to as a 'patriotic Leinsterman' and Diarmait's 'faithful propagandist'. He is recorded in the *Book of Leinster* as 'Fer léigind [lector] of the chief king of Leth Mogha Nuadat [Leinster and Munster], chief historian of Leinster in wisdom and knowledge and practice of books and learning and study.' Diarmait's chief legal expert, a hereditary position, was Ua Dorain, and the position was held in the same name four hundred years later. Mac Murchada nourished his foster family of Ua Cáellaide so carefully that one must assume that they too supported him outside his own immediate family. Dungal Ua Cáellaide became bishop of Leiglin, the western half of Uí Chennselaig. His foster brother, Áed Ua Cáellaide, was described as his chaplain, a position which no doubt provided secular as well as spiritual advice. Years later in Diarmait's foundation charter to the monastery of All Hallows in Dublin he speaks of Áed Ua Cáellaide, bishop of Louth (or Clogher) as his 'spiritual father or confessor'. Diarmait's chancellor, Florence is also named in the Latin foundation charter for the Augustinian abbey of Ferns. Neither must one overlook another man in an overseas role of power, a personal friend, the portreeve of Bristol, Robert FitzHarding. To those must be added another loyal elector of Mac Murchada kings, Ua Nualláin. In addition to these the three important office-holders were firstly the king himself, the Ua Dorain lawyer and judge and lastly Diarmait's bishop of Ferns, Ua Cattáin.

At this stage of Diarmait's career, his younger brother Murchad took a vital role in his support. He was of ruling potential himself, as he later proved, but despite this he and his brother showed none of the internecine dynastic rivalry which devastated other ruling families. There is no suspicion or suggestion of banishment, mutilation or antagonism in the brothers' relationship. Instead Murchad enjoyed the position of close adviser and executor of Diarmait's plans. He demonstrated lifelong dependability to Diarmait, a loyalty that was one of the outstanding and distinguishing attributes of his family throughout that reign.

Mac Murchada's family grew. With Sadb Ní Fáeláin he fathered another son, Donnchad, and a daughter, Órlaith.[5] Throughout the constant ebb and flow of politics and stresses, his interest in his family was sustained. Despite Diarmait's own pleasant fosterage, neither of these two children and none of his subsequent children were placed as foster children with any other family. Ferns was always their home and a training ground in which unity of purpose and cohesion was successfully inculcated. The enjoyment of relaxation at home was not, however, a luxury which detained Mac Murchada for too long.

A nominal dominance in Munster had been obtained with Thomond's Conchobar Ua Briain recognising Diarmait as overlord. Once this submission was made, Diarmait did not engage in annual conflict to maintain supremacy. This was a costly neglect. Conchobar Ua Briain without forewarning marched up to Dublin, which was now in a properous era of commerce and building, and demanded the submission of the Norsemen to the descendants of Brian Bóruma. The Norse, wondering why a hand had not been raised against the march, submitted.[6] Conchobar Ua Briain celebrated in triumph and renewed strength. From Munster he next marched into Connaught, the territory of the high king, Toirdelbach Ua Conchobair, and raided. He then raided Uí Chennselaig as far as Wexford. How or why he was not decimated remains a mystery. Whether through exertion or with excitement, Conchobar Ua Briain died within a few months. Mac Murchada pondered the audacity and came to the conclusion that a show of force must be made once more.

But with Conchobar Ua Briain's death came change. He was succeeded as king by his brother and formidable cohort, Toirdelbach Ua Briain, a man frustrated by lack of real power all his life.[7] He now possessed power and to make use of it he raided Connaught at regular intervals, looting and burning, his men encouraged by their lightning triumphs. It was more than either Diarmait or the old lion of Connaught, the high king Toirdelbach Ua Conchobair, could endure. The greater loss was Mac Murchada's, for he had lost a safe Munster. More than that, a belligerent Munster replaced it.

Mac Murchada came to an arrangement with the man for whom he had little affection, Toirdelbach Ua Conchobair.[8] Diarmait gave hostages to the high king as proof of his serious intent while arrangements were made to attack Toirdelbach Ua Briain. Diarmait marched to join the high king deep into Ua Briain's territory, but Ua Briain's men avoided the pincer movement and made a lightning raid into Diarmait's own territories. The campaign ended lamely and inconclusively but Mac Murchada had suffered loss of prestige.

Because Diarmait helped the high king and had a mutual arrangement with him, Toirdelbach Ua Conchobair again turned on Murchad Ua Máel Sechlainn, king of Meath.[9] He made him captive, even though, as the scribe recorded, 'he was under the protection of relics and guarantees of Ireland'. The high king gave the entire kingdom of Meath from the Shannon to the Irish Sea to his own son, Conchobar Ua Conchobair, the same young man he had originally created king of Leinster in 1126. This new imposition was a deed so against Irish tradition and sensibilities that the unfortunate newcomer was assassinated inside twelve months. The assassin's stated reason, which has come down across the ages, is proud: 'I considered him a stranger in sovereignty over the men of Meath'. It illustrated the terrible results of Irish diplomacy of the time.

Revenge and fury were visited upon the Meath men by Toirdelbach Ua Conchobair. A war 'like the day of Judgement' smothered their kingdom in blood and ashes and, when it was over, the west of Meath was annexed to the kingdom of Connaught and east Meath was divided in two.[10] The recipients of this latter divide were as incongruous a pair of beneficiaries as ever shared a legacy. One was married to the outraged king's daughter, Derbforgaill. His name was Tigernán Ua Ruairc of Bréifne. The other was Diarmait Mac Murchada, king of Leinster and the Norse. And both Diarmait and Ua Ruairc had nothing but hatred for each other.

If the Church had remained aloof until now, the revenge of the high king ended its isolation. The strife promulgated by Toirdelbach Ua Conchobair had festered. His action in Meath and to its king culminated in ecclesiastical intervention.[11] The most distinguished name in Ireland's Church was that of Gilla Maic Liac, archbishop of Armagh and successor of Patrick. The archbishop summoned a convention of clergy which discussed exhaustively the situation in Ireland. There were several immediate results, the most important of which was the assembly of kings, princes and laymen in Ormonde convened to persuade Toirdelbach Ua Conchobair, high king of Ireland, and Toirdelbach Ua Briain of Munster to implement the wishes of the Church. The king of Meath, Murchad Ua Máel Sechlainn, was given back his kingdom, and this was agreed by Mac Murchada. Nevertheless, as a consequence of the assassination of the high king's son, Ua Máel Sechlainn had to pay an honour fine of 400 cows and also to appoint the king's son Muirchertach as equal ruler. Diarmait and Leinster were not censured by the prelates or rulers. The two elders, Toirdelbach Ua Briain and Toirdelbach Ua Conchobair, swore an oath that they would 'make the perfect peace of Ireland so long as they should be alive.' The peace lasted a year.

As the summer of 1145 approached the four central kingdoms, Connaught, Meath, Munster and Bréifne, fought each other with such unabated fury that the recorder of the day wrote that Ireland was 'a trembling sod'.[12]

Diarmait Mac Murchada looked on and decided that there was no place for him or his Leinstermen, Irish or Norse in the strife. He did, however, intervene whenever events near his own territory threatened danger. In 1146 the ruler of Osraige, Mac Gilla Pátraic, was killed 'treacherously in the middle of Kilkenny' by the two sons of a minor chieftain, Ua Bráenáin, resulting in political upheaval in Osraige.[13] The slain king's son, Donnchad, succeeded his father while his brother, Cerball, claimed southern Osraige. Mac Murchada now directly intervened in Osraige's internal arrangements. He deposed Cerball and gave his territory

48

to Donnchad. He made a unified Osraige of respectable dimensions again. However, Donnchad proved an unreliable choice. In 1151 Mac Murchada had him arrested and restored his uncle, Cerball as king of Osraige.

Cerball was not, however, to be king of Mac Murchada's foster parents' territory. At this time the Ua Cáellaide ruler is recorded in the regnal lists of the *Book of Leinster* as reigning jointly with Mac Gilla Pátraic as king of Osraige. The Four Masters, who eventually gave Mac Murchada his horrific obituary, assure us that the king of Leinster effected these manipulations 'treacherously and with guile'. The manipulations continued. Donnchad Mac Gilla Pátraic was released by Mac Murchada and restored to his domain in northern Osraige. Cerball was shunted back to his older choice of southern Osraige.[14]

While Mac Murchada's attentions were riveted on his own borders, his enemy Ua Ruairc survived an assassination attempt which would have claimed other normal men. In 1148 a great meeting was held at the Shannon between Toirdelbach Ua Conchobair and Tigernán Ua Ruairc.[15] Here, the people of Ua Fergail fermented a conspiracy to send Tigernán Ua Ruairc to his eternal reward. A former clergyman of the Ua Fergail was elected to wield the sword, an exercise he performed with such commitment that Tigernán was horrifically mangled. Mangled but not dead. The would-be assassin was killed on the spot. Discontented with the failure of the assassination attempt, another group pursued the severely wounded Ua Ruairc in order to complete the task. They, too, lost their lives at the hands of Ua Ruairc's men. Tigernán himself recovered from his wounds to carry on, in time, his own inexhaustible bids for expansion.

SEVEN

Uí Néill Seize Power

A revitalised power now edged its way, with little warning, through thickets of enemies on to the Irish stage.[1] It succeeded in toppling Toirdelbach Ua Conchobair from the kingship of Ireland.

The red hand emblem of Ulster has been for thousands of years one of the most unusual and memorable emblems. On badges and flags, on provincial football, hurling and rugby jerseys, the blood-red hand is known as widely as the harp. No other family, either before the Norman landings or for 500 years after, made the red hand more feared or respected than the Uí Néill, the traditional ruling line of Ireland for many centuries. Now, in 1147, Muirchertach Mac Lochlainn, the Uí Néill successor to the claims to the kingship of Ireland battered his way through the north and gained the submission of three strong rulers whose armies then fought at his side. The expansion of Ua Conchobair, the high king, was at one sweep arrested. After a long lifetime of battle, the goal for which this blood was spilled, clear and unchallenged possession of all-Ireland power, was plucked from his grasp forever. It took three years of power-gathering before the northern men swarmed southwards.

The turn of events was no less critical to Diarmait Mac Murchada. His wits has been working to form an alliance which might reduce the high king and at the same time gain for himself the armies to strengthen his own position. To oppose the Uí Néill army would require an alliance with Ua Briain of Munster or Toirdelbach Ua Conchobair, but there was no hope of either facilitating Diarmait's path to power. There was only one thing to be done in the situation and that most certainly was not an alliance with two proven enemies like Toirdelbach Ua Conchobair and Toirdelbach Ua Briain. Mac Murchada had to think deeply and he had to think rapidly. Diarmait Mac Murchada, king of Leinster and the Norse, 'came into the house' of the northern king Mac Lochlainn and brought with him the strength of Leinster. The new partnership worked like a balm from the moment of its inception. Diarmait and Mac Lochlainn found their alliance so agreeable that Leinster's loyalty to the new claimant for the kingship of Ireland was permanent. In turn, Mac Lochlainn surrounded Diarmait Mac Murchada with such protection and support that his position and tenure became impregnable. Diarmait was but one step behind the most powerful man in the country. Mac Lochlainn and Mac Murchada became firm allies. The next to see the northern light was the ruler of Bréifne, Tigernán Ua Ruairc. He submitted to Mac Lochlainn, giving him recognition as high king which he withdrew from his lifelong overseer, Toirdelbach Ua Conchobair. The conditions were assembled for the last spasms in the life of the old king, Toirdelbach Ua Conchobair.

It was 1150, the first year in which Mac Lochlainn was styled king of Ireland. Submission or war were the options facing the ageing lion of Connaught. To the man of whom it is recorded that he once reduced all Ireland to 'a trembling sod', it is surprising that he only considered surrender. In Meath where Mac Lochlainn was gathered with his army, the submission and hostages of Connaught were brought to him without an upraised arm.[2] It was not that Toirdelbach Ua Conchobair was finished or that he cheerfully regarded Mac Lochlainn as his better. It was that he had nothing else to offer. It was Ua Conchobair's life and he was not yet prepared to retire but the struggle would simply never again be on so great a scale.

After Ua Conchobair's submission, or more likely as a condition for that submission, Mac Lochlainn divided the Meath kingdom of the unfortunate Murchad Ua Máel Sechlainn into three parts, while the much-banished ruler of Meath once again trod the well-beaten path to exile.[3] In this business, it is apparent that Diarmait's interest was not regarded or different arrangements might have been made. The divided kingdom of Meath was given in equal parts to the reduced Toirdelbach Ua Conchobair, Tigernán Ua Ruairc, and the northern ruler, the Ua Cerbaill of Airgialla. Mac Lochlainn was playing politics. When Mac Murchada became aware of this intrusion into an area in which he was so vitally interested, he felt outmanoeuvred, but he must have realised that it was a manoeuvre to placate the Ua Conchobair ambition rather than a gesture against himself.

Any sense of injustice was soon forgotten as Diarmait Mac Murchada became involved in one of the major confrontations of Irish history which culminated in the decisive battle of Moin Mór.[4] The story of the immediate causes of that bloody field are simply told. Toirdelbach Ua Briain survived a coup in Thomond. With restored confidence, he renewed his attempts to eliminate his Munster rival, Diarmait Mac Carthaigh, the new king of Desmond. All of Munster was involved in this new warfare. 'From Limerick to Cork, from Waterford to Brandon Hill', the whole territory was devastated. Diarmait Mac Carthaigh was routed and his only alternative to annihilation was to seek help. Diarmait Mac Murchada, to his keen interest, was approached with an urgent offer of alliance.

Whatever terms were arranged between Diarmait Mac Carthaigh and Diarmait Mac Murchada, the effects were dramatic. Mac Murchada organised the most efficient fighting force of his career to date. There were other reasons why he should risk his life before a rampant Ua Briain on his own well-surveyed territory. Mac Carthaigh had also enlisted the help of Ua Conchobair whose forces were not to be sneered at, but above all Mac Murchada had his eye on Munster for overlordship. Lastly there was the necessity to reduce a rival who shared his ambition. There was an element of retribution too for Toirdelbach Ua Briain had inflicted injuries on Leinster.

Toirdelbach Ua Conchobair still had a useful army which, though mauled by Ua Briain, was an efficient force. Mac Murchada could see a long task halved with their participation. Thus it was that Diarmait and the old war dog met once more, suspicious of one another, yet with the respect of surviving enemies. The eminence of Diarmait's position must have been a frequent cause of wonderment to the old Ua Conchobair. Twenty-five years previously he had the young Mac Murchada chased from the kingship of Leinster.

The Ua Briain army, with victory assured, was facing the battered Desmond men at Cork when it first became known that Mac Carthaig's new allies had reached the Blackwater river. They were within fifty miles. Ua Briain chose the mobile warfare he was now master of and withdrew towards his own Shannonside homeland to which he could lure and destroy the new alliance. For if he could win he would strike a mighty blow for the inheritance of Brian Bóruma.

Before Ua Briain withdrew towards Limerick, he ransacked the town of Cork. On his withdrawal, however, he was pursued by Mac Carthaigh and the Desmond men who read retreat into his move. The essential element for the military commander, luck, escaped Toirdelbach Ua Briain for the first time. The day of Ua Briain's withdrawal was shrouded in a dense fog and the battalions of Thomond marched straight into the middle of the Mac Murchada and the Ua Conchobair armies. The collision of forces took place at the grassy plain known as Moin Mór. It was a savage battle. The characteristic by which Mac Murchada was to become renowned made itself apparent. His voice could carry over the din of battle and, as the conflict wore on, his voice grew hoarse, yet audible, as he shouted orders and encouragement to his men. This roaring figure of Irish warfare could also be heard by the enemy and as the hard day wore on his urgings increased.

The battalions of Thomond gave way and slaughter ensued. The aftermath was recorded. As Mac Murchada's men and the Connaught men lurched back from the field, they were assailed by the cries of the wounded, dying and mutilated. They had won. A witness of the black day for the south contributed for posterity in the *Annals of Tigernach:*

Until sand of sea and stars of heaven are numbered, no one will reckon all the sons of kings and chiefs and great lords of the men of Munster that were killed there, so that of the three great divisions of Munstermen that had come there none of them escaped except only one shattered division.

The Miscellaneous Irish Annals and the Four Masters relapse into less poetic detail. They number the Munster dead at 7,000. Toirdelbach Ua Briain himself with a few horsemen escaped from the battlefield, undetected through the fog, and they whipped their horses away northwards across the river. Ua Briain of Thomond's last blow for all-Ireland power was over.

EIGHT

Mac Murchada Prestige

By the middle of the twelfth century Mac Murchada was one of the most dominent figures in Ireland, and with the shield of the high king Mac Lochlainn he had also become the most secure. His reputation was never higher. His shrewdness had achieved political progress in a kingdom of two distinct races and many clashing personalities. His bravery and his spirit were renowned. Particularly his spirit in adversity, for his recovery from a disastrous start was one of the achievements of the century. Its effect was to arouse expansionist policies in the major Irish ruling families to a new crescendo when obstacles to ambition were usually emasculated or reduced with haste. Ua Ruairc underestimated him as a youth. Later, in 1141, Mac Murchada had pounced before his rivals could draw sword. It was unfortunate that the major ruling families' expansion occurred at the same time and in a period when they were of equal strength. With all of them, the unending spur to expand their own territory and power was the predominant political urge. For the time being the fortunes of the Norse were bound up with their own overlords, as long as they considered it advantageous.

Most of Mac Murchada's achievements had been gained without an annual sacrifice of blood from his people. This was one of the factors which marked him out to thinking men as a man of accomplishment. However alone, without allies, he was not strong enough, and this, too, was known. His strength lay in his own personality, his complex, searching, feverishly working character.

At this time of intense political manoeuvring for Mac Murchada, he became involved in a máelstrom of ecclesiastical upheavals which had momentous and unsuspected significance for himself and for Ireland. They must be looked at in chronological order.

At this period a phenomenon infused Christendom. The name of this phenomenon was Bernard, the abbot of the Cistercian monastery of Clairvaux in western France. His voice pierced the ears of all, from Armagh to Antioch, who leaned toward any pull of the flesh. From the cloister of the French hinterland he unleashed a whirlwind of reform. His Pentecostal authority lashed with equal vigour the inept, the criminal, the rogue and the corrupt. On one occasion he issued a tongue-lashing to the pontiff himself. His fundamental honesty attracted thousands to him and his harsh rule of life. Bernard gained a spiritual ambassador in Ireland, a towering figure in the Irish Church, Malachy, retired archbishop of Armagh and primate of All Ireland, papal legate, and then bishop of Down.

In 1140 Malachy visited the monastery of Clairvaux on his return journey from Rome in July and August.[1] He left four young men behind him in Clairvaux, while others were taught the Cistercian rules in other abbeys for eventual transfer to Ireland. Malachy returned obsessed with the urgency of reform in Ireland and was a determined disciple of Bernard. He dispatched more Irish aspirants to Clairvaux. One was of particular significance. Gilla Críst Ua Connairche, from Bangor, was appointed the father superior of the Irish monks in training in France. He was to become one of the most dominant of the twelfth-century intriguers for Christ. Malachy had long grasped the significance of Bernard. So did the monarchs of Brehon Ireland, for no Christian land was remote enough to ignore the rage of his tongue.

Church history was made and influenced by Clairvaux. Bernard himself launched the first crusade against the Moslems by his oratory. And from this place an even greater phenomenon was created, for in 1145 a mild monk from Clairvaux, a close confrère of Gilla Críst Ua Connairche, was elected to the throne of St Peter on the very day the old pope had died.[2] A Cistercian monk of Bernard's abbey was pope. He took the name of Eugenius III.

Malachy had by this time introduced the Cistercians into Ireland. The first foundation was at Mellifont and its first abbot was the recalled Gilla Críst Ua Connairche. Malachy, who originally had the idea of reforming the Church in Ireland, also introduced the Canons Regular of St Augustine with Bernard's commendation.[3] Like the Cistercians, the Augustinians were propelled by Bernard. Their reforming power house was at Arrouaise in France. Their recruits included women, and Augustinian convents of the Arrouaisian discipline branched out from France. Malachy, who had also inspected Arrouaise, decided that Ireland could use some of the women who responded to the spirit and the letter of the Augustinian rule and so they too were invited to form a bridgehead. By the middle of the twelfth century the institutions of the Church in Ireland were being infiltrated, and eventually dominated, by men and women determined on reform, but trained in a different and hostile culture, namely France.

Diarmait Mac Murchada involved himself in matters ecclesiastical. In 1146 he made his first foundation. From the selection open to him he chose to found a house for the nuns of the Arrouaise Augustinian rule and to locate the foundation at Dublin. It was named St Mary de Hogges, with the rank of abbey. Whether urged by ecclesiastical diplomacy, or by conviction, Diarmait Mac Murchada became infected by the reforming ideal, despite his uncanonical private life, and being sworn to defend the Brehon society to which he was heir. When he considered the erection of an abbey of appropriate size and impact in his home ruling area, he had two reforming orders in mind. These two were the Cistercians and the Canons Regular of St Augustine. This time he selected the Cistercians and looked to the abbot of Mellifont, Gilla Críst Ua Connairche, to provide the first monks. The site he selected for the new abbey was Baltinglass, at the sloping toes of the great Wicklow mountains, alongside the Slaney river. Diarmait formally founded the abbey in 1148 and it was called the abbey de Valle Salutis. Baltinglass abbey, and its outstanding abbots, such as Máel Ísu Ua Laighenáin and Ailbe Ua Máel Muaid, were to have their own impact on Ireland's political and ecclesiastical history.

The cloister never concealed the fact that Bernard of Clairvaux was the most powerful churchman in Christendom. His thoughts did not neglect Ireland. The reform he had ignited had gathered pace and those who nurtured the seed were cherished in his heart. He was in constant communication with his brethren and they in turn communicated the advances, the setbacks, the accomplishments, the benefactors. Ireland was a missionary ground of promise. Diarmait Mac Murchada swiftly advanced in the warm glow of approval. Bernard assessed his reception and patronage of the Cistercian Order and ultimately his contribution and stature won him an enormous prize, not shared by any of his peers. Mac Murchada won the accolade of the written benefaction of Bernard of Clairvaux himself. Bernard composed a precious letter in Latin and had it delivered to Diarmait Mac Murchada:[4]

> *A letter from the community to Diarmait, king of Ireland. Bernard, abbot of Clairvaux, sends greetings and good wishes to the noble and glorious king of Ireland.*
>
> *Your renown has reached this country, and we rejoice exceedingly in the good reports of you: that you received with regal generosity the poor of Christ – or rather, Christ Himself in the persons of these poor. It is truly a matter of amazement to us that a king who reigns over a barbarous people should pursue the works of mercy with such generosity. Those whom you have welcomed are our own very offspring, and you may cherish yourself in them and regard them as your own.*
>
> *Accordingly, we thank your regal majesty, praying for you and for your kingly salvation, that the Lord our God may give you peace in your days. And that you may carry out more freely and more completely what you have initiated, we make you a participant in all the good works which we perform in our house and our order, and we pray that when you depart your kingdom, it will be for an eternal one.*

This epistle stirred noble emotions in Diarmait Mac Murchada. While the description of his people as 'barbarous' may have stifled his joy, the happily chosen reference to him as 'king of Ireland' overwhelmed his distaste. 'King of Ireland!' To be contemplated thus by the most eminent ecclesiastic in Christendom was a magnificent gain. Whatever can be read into Bernard's address, the germ of ambition which required little stimulation gathered strength in Mac Murchada.

Time inched past, important changes accumulated, the significance of which only became apparent with the passage of time. One such dramatic change occurred in Mac Murchada's sphere of influence in Norse Waterford. Friction in the Church between the Norse diocese of Waterford and the Irish diocese of neighbouring Lismore was increasing. When the aged bishop of Lismore died in 1150 the question of the successor to such turmoil was crucial. On the Holy Father's own lips there tripped the name of that man. The Cisterican pope appointed the northern Cistercian abbot of Mellifont, his one-time confrere, Gilla Críst Ua Connairche, to the Atlantic coast see of Lismore,[5] where he remained for one of the most eventful episcopal reigns in Irish history. A Holy watchdog, a watchdog who could report to the Holy See every indiscreet breach of any commandment, was installed at Mac Murchada's side.

Mac Murchada's spiritual enterprise continued. In 1150 he subordinated the convents of Kilculliheen in Osraige near Waterford city, and Aghade in modern county Carlow to the Arrouaisian abbey of St Mary de Hogges in Dublin.[6] Both assumed the rank of priory. Still there was an urgent need to regularise the Church in Ireland. That was finally tackled two years later when a great synod was convened. To the men whose lives were consecrated to God, 1152 was a light beaming at the end of a dim cloister. A full national synod whose agenda was unambiguous, was held at Kells.[7]

It was to promote the Catholic faith; to purify and to correct the morals of the people; to consecrate four archbishops and to give them the pallia.

The Holy Father, Eugenius III, well briefed, sent a legate from Rome to the synod. He was His Eminence Giovanni Cardinal Paparo, cardinal priest of St Lawrence in Damaso. The Holy Father also elevated the Cistercian bishop of Lismore to the rank of papal legate to Ireland. Gilla Críst Ua Connairche. From then on he was the eyes and ears of the vicar of Christ in Ireland, and few known transgressions went unrecorded or untransmitted.

In resolve and Church government the synod was an outstanding success. The royal heads of Ireland gave approval to every one of the decrees issued. It is doubtful if they gave enthusiastic assent to the decrees on Christian marriage which were spartan by comparison with Brehon Law, but the prelates had no choice but to pass decrees outlawing concubinage and irregular unions.

Instead of two archbishops – Cashel and Armagh – four were now admitted and the pallium conferred on the occupants. The two new archepiscopal sees were Tuam and Dublin. Dublin was Norse and its situation was awkward. The Norse had little regard for the Irish Church and had their bishops consecrated by Canterbury. The synod of Kells might have declared the see of Glendalough worthy of the pallium, but it observed the influence over powerful Norse Dublin by Leinster and found it politic to offer the honour to Gregory, bishop of Dublin. The Norse estrangement from the Irish Church ended at once with Gregory's acceptance.

In the political arena the most welcome event was the acceptance of Muirchertach Mac Lochlainn of Cenél nEógain as high king 'without opposition'.[8] It was startling only in contrast to years of Ua Conchobair strength. In this year Mac Lochlainn's chief obstacle to the high kingship, Toirdelbach Ua Conchobair, the former high king, made ultimate lasting peace with him.

In this year the two most powerful kings in Ireland, Muir-chertach Mac Lochlainn and Toirdelbach Ua Conchobair, met and made friendship under the staff of Jesus and under the relics of Columcille.[9]

It is not recorded who brought them together but the only person linking the two with the prestige to be a negotiator was Diarmait Mac Murchada. Immediately after the formal peace was made, Mac Murchada joined the other two rulers for the first time to legislate for all Ireland. The king of Leinster, in conference with Ua Conchobair and Mac Lochlainn, readjusted the boundaries of the battered kingdom of Meath. In this resettlement, Mac Murchada exercised strong influence, for his friends, the Ua Máel Sechlainn of Meath, at last came into their own. Tigernán Ua Ruairc was removed from the overlordship of partitioned Meath granted to him previously.[10] These events confirm Diarmait's now national importance and suggest that it was perhaps he who arranged the union of Muirchertach Mac Lochlainn and Toirdelbach Ua Conchobair.

Diarmait regarded Mac Lochlainn highly. He was, however, no Brian Bóruma and he made no attempt to gain power over the whole country but seemed content with the honour of the title alone. He didn't develop the position of the high kingship, which had remained the same since the battle of Clontarf in 1014. Mac Lochlainn was the strongest sword, not the great ruler that the country needed.

Of the old friends in this hierarchy, no one was regarded by Diarmait Mac Murchada with the same intimacy and sympathy as Murchad Ua Máel Sechlainn, the ruler of Meath. If Mac Murchada depended on his allies' support for his continued health, what may be said of Murchad Ua Máel Sechlainn? Without Diarmait Mac Murchada's constant and repeated care, Ua Máel Sechlainn would have long been dead, his buffer state a memory. It was in Ua Máel Sechlainn's home that Diarmait could relax without one eye focused on an adversary. It was with Murchad Ua Máel Sechlainn and his family that plans and futures could be discussed and power shifts assessed. It was within this alliance of families that Diarmait knew Ua Máel Sechlainn's daughter, Derbforgaill, now married to the man they both regarded as the personification of barbarity, Tigernán Ua Ruairc.

Even the most mobile of the twelfth-century kings in Ireland found that there were periods when they rested their swords, relaxed, defeated or satisfied. Not so Tigernán Ua Ruairc. Great difficulty will be found in naming one year in Ua Ruairc's reign when he did not stride into conflict. It was as if he regarded the predecessors in his line as idlers to make up for whose indolence he had to work with demonic zeal. Despite this, Ua Ruairc of Bréifne has escaped the curse of the Gael. He has rather emerged from history as a benign old gentlemen whose dutiful young wife was stolen screaming from him. It is one of the extraordinary turnabouts of history that the curses have fallen upon Mac Murchada. Despite the fact that Ua Ruairc was married to Derbforgaill, the daughter of Meath's ruler, he lost no opportunity terrorise it. Whenever Meath was about to be carved up, Ua Ruairc was there determined to take his share of land or to inflict pain on Ua Máel Sechlainn. How his life was spared to old age is a mystery. Mac Murchada did not consider him worth blinding when he trounced him. Yet from numerous defeats he returned to brawl and scourge to his dying day.

It must be said, however, that Meath was the key to all-Ireland power. So many were occupied in trying to conquer and absorb this territory that this ensured its survival through many changes. To Mac Murchada, to Ua Ruairc, to Ua Cerbaill, to Ua Conchobair and to Mac Lochlainn, Meath was the golden fleece, the undisputed possession of which meant not only power, but wealth, for here more than anywhere else in Ireland, grass, the basic wealth producer, could grow on the timber shaft of a cart. Its central position, its proximity to Dublin, its possession of the root of mystic Gaelic power, Tara, made its absorption central to the power starved. Ua Ruairc, who was awarded an area of Meath two years previously, was now dismissed from it. So were Ua Conchobair and Ua Cerbaill, who accepted the restoration of Ua Máel Sechlainn.

The new settlement restored the entire kingdom of Meath to the Ua Máel Sechlainn with this one alteration: Murchad Ua Máel Sechlainn, Diarmait's friend, was restored to the western half of Meath next to Connaught and bounded by the Shannon. His son, Máel Sechlainn Ua Máel Sechlainn, was put in charge of the eastern part of Meath which ended at the Irish Sea. To Tigernán Ua Ruairc, the prospect of being reduced northwestwards back to the beautiful lakes of his family's enclave, did not appeal. The ruler of Bréifne, in a fury like a bull driven from a field packed with heifers, saw the hand of Mac Murchada thwarting his right to breathe. He denounced and defied the high king, king of Leinster and, firing hammer after anvil, included in his malediction his wife's family, the Ua Máel Sechlainn of Meath. Meath was Ua Ruairc's and no one had the right to take it away.

Mac Murchada felt a lifelong hatred for Ua Ruairc. It sprang from the time Ua Ruairc injured the pride of a young Mac Murchada. The wheel had turned a full cycle. Now Ua Ruairc, who had a lifetime of experience and could not be excused by the fever of youth, was defying the rule of law established and accepted by all Ireland. The time had come for Mac Murchada to feed himself on the old grudge. Should he be blinded? Hanged? Handed over perhaps to Ua Máel Sechlainn? Or would all those simple exercises be too easy?

NINE

The Wife of Tigernán Ua Ruairc

Women in twelfth-century Ireland did not play a public, prominent role. The record is so empty of them that one could conclude that they were of but modest significance. That, as experience shows, would be a serious error. In the middle of that century one woman came to major prominence. To this day she is the woman still known nationally because of her association with the king of Leinster, Diarmait Mac Murchada. She is the only woman associated in the public mind with the pre-Norman years and she is regarded by some as partly responsible for upheavals in later decades. These however are nothing more than perceptions.

Derbforgaill Ua Máel Sechlainn was born in 1108. She was the daughter of Murchad, king of Meath. Of her early years very little is known. She first came to quiet notice when she was married to Tigernán Ua Ruairc, king of Bréifne in 1128. Ua Ruairc's territory is approximately the same as that of the diocese of Kilmore today in the province of Armagh. Derbforgaill's sister, Tailtu, was married to Toirdelbach Ua Conchobair, king of Connaught.

The mixture of cunning political play with sexual involvement is not a recent phenomenon but perhaps it was exercised with greater intensity in the 1100s than it is now. Both factors were to contribute in Derbforgaill's movements on the national scene. Her prominence, though brief, has inspired poets, writers, playwrights and historians. There was an established relationship between Derbforgaill and Diarmait Mac Murchada. Diarmait's great secretary, Ó Regan, tells of frequent messages and love letters from Mac Murchada to Derbforgaill with one aim: revenge on Ua Ruairc for his humiliation. The reduction of Ua Ruairc in his declining years was a matter of fact while the ascendancy to national honour of her family's friend, Mac Murchada, was plainly obvious.

Through her family she had lifelong knowledge of Diarmait as a man and she also knew of the implacable hatred of Diarmait for Ua Ruairc. It was a hatred which disregarded all barriers.

Then came the Ua Máel Sechlainn intervention in 1152. She persuaded her brother, Máel Sechlainn Ua Máel Sechlainn of Meath, to support her plan. He sent a letter to the king of Leinster acquainting him of his sister's repudiation of Ua Ruairc, instigating Diarmait to the deed 'for some abuses of her husband Tigernán, done to her before'[1] and informing him of Derbforgaill's consent to bestowing on Mac Murchada the rewards the conjugation would provide.

Diarmait Mac Murchada is recorded as having been married three if not four times. It is not certain whether he was married to more than one woman at the same time or if he was married to one woman alone in each case. It is also not clear whether he remarried on the death of a partner or after separation following a previous arrangement. A plurality of wives or partnerships in concubinage, no less than monogamous marriage, were eventualities all catered for under the Brehon code and no stress whatever was inflicted on the body politic over them provided the bilateral honour compensation stipulations were adhered to. Diarmait Mac Murchada through both marriage and liaison now had a thriving family of offspring in Ferns.[2] Domnall Cáemánach Mac Murchada, his first son, had matured and was markedly in possession of all his father's instincts, ambitions, loyalty and capabilities. Diarmait's first wife Sadb, the daughter of the king of Uí Fáeláin, had given him a son, Donnchad, and a daughter, Órlaith. He had two other children whose mother's name is not recorded, so whether they were from a second marriage or from another enterprise is not certain. One was a son, Énna, and the second a daughter, Derbforgaill. Both were children of outstanding promise and potential.

Contented with his family, famed in his accomplishments, cushioned with loyal guards and possessing uncommon wit, Mac Murchada was now subjected to a remarkable twist of fate. What appeared to be satisfaction and the thorough humiliation of an enemy, developed into ghastly mistake. Yet as the prospect opened itself before Mac Murchada's eyes, every step was logical, the right one to grasp, the sure path to revenge and power.

When Mac Murchada received word from Ua Máel Sechlainn, he must have felt elated. He had everything. Here was Bréifne's wife, an Ua Máel Sechlainn of Meath. Here was revenge, an enemy's humiliation and ruin, all compressed into one executed enterprise. This was it. This was the revenge he sought. He would reduce Ua Ruairc, but he would let him live, and live to face the grins of men. He would take his wife, a wife who would leave Ua Ruairc of her own free will. She would walk away with Ua Ruairc's destroyer. Revenge with its advances in power was at last vouchsafed to Mac Murchada; and hell blast reform, Cistercians, and Augustinians too.

Ua Ruairc's army was savaged. With the impatience of unfulfilled destruction Mac Murchada flailed Ua Ruairc's kingdom. To make revenge even more bitter Mac Murchada was joined by Toirdebach Ua Conchobair in the thorough destruction of Ua Ruairc. When the bloody campaign was over, Ua Ruairc's fortress at Dangan in modern county Roscommon was razed to the ground. His own territory was halved and the most fertile portion of it Conmaicne which today comprises county Longford and the southern part of county Leitrim, was bestowed on a more docile member of the Ua Ruairc family, Gilla Braite Ua Ruairc. Ua Ruairc himself was left alive in a bewildered daze, groping for swords and finding nothing. He was left with only his wife Derbforgaill. What of Derbforgaill? Mac Murchada now contemplated the prize. No longer a girl with romance leaping through her head, her offer of herself to Mac Murchada is one of the most intriguing events in Irish history. She was part of a culture wherein her repudiation of a husband and her offer of herself to another man were not without precedent or approval. Everything by Brehon Law usage was in order, but it strictly stipulated that an appropriate honour price be paid to the injured husband.

Accompanied by a group of mounted men Mac Murchada went

to where Derbforgaill waited. One of his men took her with him on his horse. At this Derbforgaill commenced to scream hysterically, to weep and struggle. The party turned heel and with Derbforgaill screaming in protest commenced the long journey back to Ferns.[3] Mac Murchada's permanent aide, Maurice Ó Regan, added the epitaph to the phase of life that followed: 'She was a fair and lovely lady, entirely beloved of Diarmait'.

In addition to Derbforgaill, Derbforgaill's cattle and furniture were also taken back to Ferns. There was one final gesture to be made by law of the land. The honour price for Derbforgaill to Ua Ruairc. It was here that Mac Murchada chose to ignore the law. He chose instead to add a last cut of the whip to Tigernán Ua Ruairc. No honour price was paid for Derbforgaill.

Derbforgaill's exhibition of protest had seen to it that there had been no public humiliation of Ua Ruairc. Her screams were also an insurance against any unexpected outcome to the adventure. It now appeared to all, except Diarmait and the Ua Máel Sechlainns, that it was a case of abduction and rape. If this was so, it was without recent precedent, for the Brehon Laws, though lax by Church standards, were nevertheless the more strongly binding because they were reasonable. Diarmait could hardly put the blame for his seduction of Derbforgaill on her when pressure was later applied to him. And he certainly could not plead innocence, for the maximum damage to Ua Ruairc was his motive.

The affair, as it appeared to the Church leaders, was shameful as it dashed their hopes not only in Mac Murchada but in the easier implementation of the decrees of the synod of Kells. It was not an affair between a cowherd and milkmaid. It was an act of theft and rape by a king, one of the greatest names in the country who was expected to lead by example. This was how it was viewed from the abroad and all over Ireland. The two major kings, Toirdelbach Ua Conchobair in his declining years, and the high king, Muirchertach Mac Lochlainn, both held the same view since no honour price was paid. Yet so great was Mac Murchada's stature that no one lifted a finger against him at the time.

He brought his new find slowly from Bréifne across the flat central plain towards the soft blue slopes of the Blackstairs mountain range and *Sliabh Buídhe*. The flatness of the central plain makes the heights heroic and as Diarmait and his party broke through the passes down into the haven of Uí Chennselaig surrounding Ferns, the shelter banished all thoughts of danger, all thoughts of aftermath. The idea that the event could be extended to a national outrage was too absurd to be contemplated.

Derbforgaill came to Ferns and remained there. She was followed later by her cattle, walked all the way from Bréifne, a satisfactory addition of wealth to the capital of Ferns. It is difficult to fathom her. She was an extremely clever woman. Her later life is a model of wifely docility and charitable works. Was it that she wanted one hour in the centre of the stage? Was it that she wanted Mac Murchada, the family friend, known from girlhood, the admired success? Or did she want to further undermine Ua Ruairc? Apart from the resulting strifes, no record exists of the affair's progress from Diarmait's recorders or Derbforgaill's lips.

While the much publicised and dramatised tryst between Diarmait and Derbforgaill extended from 1152 into the following year a much less known liaison was being nourished by Diarmait Mac Murchada. In that same period negotiations or, if you will, formal courtship, was initiated by the king of Leinster with another woman. The focus of Mac Murchada's attention, or affection, was Mór Ua Tuathail, only daughter of the king of Uí Muíredaig and Uí Mail.[4] This territory, ruled by the Ua Tuathail, extended approximately from Powerscourt in county Wicklow south to Castledermot and from Glendalough to Athy. It straddled Leinster on the approaches to Dublin.

The Ua Tuathail dynasty had been antagonistic to Mac Murchada. The recent dominance of Uí Chennselaig added to their disrespect, the more so in that their weakness frustrated Ua Tuathail efforts to loosen Mac Murchada's hold on Leinster. On Mac Murchada's restoration to military health he made the Ua

Tuathail territory a target for dominance. That was duly procured and the contract was solidified with a hostage. The hostage was by any standard an important person. His name was Lorcán Ua Tuathail. The death of Lorcáns brother, Ugaire, a few years previously while doing battle for Mac Murchada did nothing to improve relations between the two families. It is likely that Ugaire fought under duress while Lorcán was held captive as insurance for Ua Tuathail compliance. Nevertheless a benign relationship had developed between Mac Murchada and his hostage.

Meanwhile, while Derbforgaill sheltered in Ferns, unions deemed illicit by the Church had come under sustained attack. Cardinal John Paparo had declared at the synod at Kells that 'kinswomen and concubines should be put away by men'. The papal legate would have met the principal kings as a matter of course, amongst them the king of Leinster. The cardinal granted confirmation of a charter issued by Diarmait to the Augustinian nunnery of Aghade in modern county Carlow. The brazen audacity and political skills of Diarmait Mac Murchada are fascinating to study, whether or not you admire the consequences of his actions.

The events of 1152 in the king of Leinster's life did not deflect the two senior royal heads, Mac Lochlainn and Ua Conchobair, from indicating to Mac Murchada that the outrage heaped on Ua Ruairc honour so completely against the Brehon law, would not be countenanced. Indeed Ua Ruairc himself began to feel once more the merest hope of regeneration. He, formally and with humility, submitted to the ailing Toirdelbach Ua Conchobair of Connaught and, from the tattered remnants of his family and warriors gave him hostages for his good behaviour. Ua Ruairc's hostages were safe because Ua Ruairc would not have been capable of raiding an orchard.

Mac Murchada had had plenty of time to interpret Derbforgaill's protests. He may have felt emotions ranging from cynicism and revulsion to indifference or he may have felt sufficiently satisfied. Far from raising an objection to the demands for her return, he facilitated the departure of what had become an inconvenient nuisance. To the expedition in 1153 of Ua Conchobair no hand was raised even when it was deep in Diarmait's kingdom. He met Ua Conchobair's expedition with Derbforgaill at Old Gowlin on the slopes of the Blackstairs facing the west and handed her over. There is no account of tears or screams.[5]

In addition to her person, her cattle, their increase, and her furniture were given back, and the procession withdrew to the central plain on their journey to the lakes of Bréifne. There was an insult offered by Diarmait. Whether it was an insult offered to his recent amour or an insult to the injured Ua Ruairc of Bréifne is a matter for interpretation. The fact remained that with the return of Derbforgaill and her cattle, he still refused to pay the honour fine laid down by the Brehon law as owed to the injured husband. The joust with Derbforgaill took no sting out of Mac Murchada, and one is tempted to think that she discovered a man little different in attention to political strife than her husband.

Despite what was perceived as a scandal in Ferns relations between Mac Murchada and the Ua Tuathail family became warm, if not close. In 1153 Lorcán Ua Tuathail, brother of Mór and once Mac Murchada's hostage, became abbot of the major monastic complex of Glendalough. To achieve that position the sponsorship of Mac Murchada as king of Leinster is taken for granted.

The proposal of marriage to Mór Ua Tuathail was accepted. Whatever else it was a political masterstroke. In such a situation could one not expect alliance for the future?

In 1153 or 1154, the exact date is not known, the marriage between Diarmait and Mór took place. Although the rest of her life was momentous and later tragic, her role was concealed in silence. No scandal, no repudiation, no drama is associated with her name. She remains noted by history only as the canonically married, principal wife of Diarmait Mac Murchada, king of Leinster and the Norse, sister of Lorcán Ua Tuathail, archbishop of Dublin, primate of Ireland.

Derbforgaill returned to what appeared to be a life of docility. Four years after her return to her husband she is noted in 1157 amongst the gathering of kings, nobles and prelates at the consecration of Ireland's first Cistercian abbey at Mellifont. She made a gift to the abbey of sixty ounces of gold, a gold chalice for the Blessed Virgin's altar, and nine cloths for the other altars of the church.

The ceaselessly active Mac Murchada found time in a nerve-draining 1153 to take part in a struggle to decide who should be king of Thomond. To that ground-covering project he added a minor atrocity nearer home. He held in fetters one of his subordinate rulers. He was Ó Mórdha, ruler of Laoighis, suspected associate of Mac Murchada's inveterate foe, Mac Gilla Pátraic, king of Osraige. Before the year was out he had been blinded and in this state released from his fetters, 'against the guarantee of laity and clergy'.[6]

Sure enough, as the pessimist would say, judgement began to visit the major actors in the Derbforgaill drama. Derbforgaill's father, who had survived a dozen invasions, banishments, dethronings and restorations, finally succumbed in the wake of his daughter's seduction of Mac Murchada.[7] His son Máel Sechlainn Ua Máel Sechlainn with whom he had shared the kingdom of Meath and who had been the *agent d'amour* between Diarmait and Derbforgaill, now inherited the entire kingdom of Meath as his own. To remove the main aspirant to part of his kingdom, Ua Máel Sechlainn now blinded his own nephew, the son of his elder brother. Further, the Four Masters, no publicists of Mac Murchada's credits, indicate that Ua Failge and Uí Fáeláin were transferred from his grip to Meath.

Diarmait's power was subjected to abrupt and tragic losses. He and Sadb Ua Fáeláin's son, Donnchad Mac Murchada, was killed by Mac Gilla Pátraic's Osraige men at Cell Draignech in Uí Dróna. A sharp, punishing raid by the Osraige antagonists sliced into Diarmait's core homeland as venom thrived between them.[8] It was a raiding expedition that would have been wiped out three years previously when Mac Murchada had Mac Gilla Pátraic under tight control. Nor was that all. From the bogs of Bréifne the trounced Ua Ruairc shook the mud off his coat and from the chasm of his despair decided to pluck a hair from Mac Murchada's beard. He made a lightning raid down into Diarmait's new wife's home territory in central Leinster and withdrew unscathed.

Nevertheless, time moved on and the memory of loss and the Derbforgaill machinations seemed to recede. There was again a period of peace made all the more comfortable by Ua Briain of Munster giving hostages to the ailing Toirdelbach Ua Conchobair of Connaught. The only tidal wave recorded was caused by the necessity for the high king Mac Lochlainn to impress upon Ua Conchobair that the name of Ireland's high king was Mac Lochlainn. To make this impression a formidable one, he hired ships and men from the coast of Scotland, Arran, Man and Cantyre to oppose an Ua Conchobair fleet.[9]

There was another development which gathered speed, fostered in the heart of Church prelates. Their helplessness in the face of Brehon society had been replaced by the knowledge that a new order was being spread throughout Europe, Asia Minor and Britain by French arms. This facility with the sword promised that in the Norman French-dominated lands the necessary ecclesiastical reforms would be securely implemented.[10] The papal legate, the bishop of Lismore, Gilla Críst Ua Connairche adopted this position in Ireland. He was a man encouraged by the synod of Kells, a man heartened at the Cistercian foundation by Mac Murchada in Baltinglass. He was revolted by the farce enacted between Derbforgaill and the king of Leinster, with whom he enjoyed cordial relations. Gilla Críst grasped that political order under the Norman-French system was in the interest of religion. Other prelates accepted the same view but the most zealous and tireless of the reformers were found among the French-trained Cistercians.

TEN

The World Scene

The map of Europe and North Africa in the mid-1100s was exciting. It showed promise of fascinating development in the years ahead, as it had showed alteration in the previous hundred years. As ever, there were two powers on the periphery of greatness, and there were those on the decline.

The great powers were the German Empire, which extended from Denmark to Rome and whose kaiser was styled the Holy Roman Emperor; and the Byzantine, Greek or western Roman Empire, with its capital in Constantinople, today's Istanbul. The powers in decline were firstly the Moslems (who, nevertheless, still occupied, after 400 years, most of Spain and Portugal, in addition to North Africa and the Middle East) and the Principality of Russia, which was seemingly irrevocably split in 1139.

It was the Normans who came unheralded from obscurity to an inheritance which, in Diarmait Mac Murchada's lifetime, extended from the Irish Sea to Antioch in Asia Minor, and from northern France to Syracuse. In England they had infiltrated a Saxon-Norse jigsaw in one of the great seaborne invasions of the era. The rest of Europe bore a striking resemblance to the divisions we know today. There were the strong kingdoms of Sweden, Denmark and Norway. In 1130 the king of Norway's writ still ran round threequarters of the coast of Scotland. Poland was in almost the exact position it occupies today after 800 years of boundary shifts, expansion and decline. Hungary controlled its present area with a significant outlet on the Adriatic Sea in modern Croatia. Germany's bulk straddled Europe while the confederation of Russian princes was bound together by an alliance as loose and permanent as a similar Irish arrangement. In the eastern Roman Empire, or modern Greece, Christ was king. The ruler there, the 'equal of the apostles', was merely His deputy. To the south across the Mediterranean were those regarded as the anti-Christs, the Moslems.

In addition to their adopted motherland in Normandy the Normans controlled neighbouring Brittany, England, all Italy south of Rome, Sicily, several crusader enclaves and they created kingdoms in modern Syria and Israel. Most remarkably of all, the conquests of the Normans in southern Italy were consolidated by Roger of Sicily who elevated the state he had built when he incorporated the Zirid emirates of Tunisia into his kingdom between 1134 and 1153. 'In wealth and civilisation his court rivalled that of Constantinople.'

Who were these Normans who achieved so much under the noses of the long-established world powers? They were men from a single province of France, Normandy a province not much greater in extent than Mac Murchada's sphere of interest in Ireland. To any Irish citizen who avails of the opportunity to visit Normandy, there is a discovery waiting. Normandy, except for its cities like Rouen or Caen, is like their homeland in climate, foliage, grasses, trees, farm enterprises and roads. It is a province which had suffered from the early Viking raids as Ireland had. And in much the same way it received its flood of Norse settlers.

The distinct history of Normandy, just like Dublin's, starts with the permanent settling of the Norse. This Norse distinction was cemented when their leader, Rolf, a man who had created havoc in raids in Ireland, was declared ruler of Normandy, early in the tenth century by the king, Charles III. Unlike Ireland, where the Norse remained in the city states, the Norman Norse were assimilated and the influences of their harsh foundation stock became a dominant characteristic when they first burst out of their confines. If there was any tradition of apartheid between the native Normans and the Norse, it was rapidly eroded inside of one hundred years. The men who conquered from 1050 to the late 1100s were French in ideas, culture and orientation.

The Normans as seen by an Italian, Geoffrey Malaterra, at the time of their Italian adventures are interesting. He says:

The Normans are a cunning and revengeful people; eloquence and dissimilation appear to be their hereditary qualities. They can stoop to flatter; but unless they are curbed by the restraint of law they indulge the licentiousness of nature or passion. Their princes affect the praise of popular munificence; the people blend the extremes of avarice and prodigality, and in their eager thirst of wealth and dominion, they despise whatever they possess and hope whatever they desire. Arms and horses, the luxury of dress, the exercise of hunting and hawking are the delight of the Normans; but on pressing occasions they can endure with incredible patience the inclemency of every climate and the toil and abstinence of a military life.

The Normans were fortunate in their leaders from William the Conqueror onwards. Talented men, fired by greed, they produced no weaklings at the helm, and though many of these overseas barons could well have proclaimed himself the equal or superior of his own monarch, yet the ties of race maintained a discipline.

The pope was, as vicar of Christ, the moral power in Christendom. But the human material in the see of Peter was frequently as frail as the times were ruthless. In 1118 a lawless Roman aristocrat, Frangipani, could slap the pontiff into a dungeon after his troops had trodden him with their spurs. Then there was the shame of Christendom. The anti-pope, a rival claimant to the see of Peter.

In 1120 the growing influence of the French was manifested in the election of a Frenchman to the papal throne. He took the name of Callistus II. He was Archbishop Guy, a recognised scholar with royal blood. The new pope, who won the support of all the Latin powers, restored the prestige of the papacy. Pope Callistus also won German loyalty, even though their emperor had backed the anti-pope. Within one year he had restored the rightful papacy to a state of honour. The Normans looked after the anti-pope. They captured him in his Roman villa, persuaded him to acknowledge his error and deposited him in a monastery. Despite occasional machinations from Roger, the Norman king of Sicily, the Normans became from then on sturdy upholders of papal authority.

No monarch in Christendom could occupy his throne unless he

had it with the good will of the pope. And the giving and taking away of power and thrones was an acknowledged property of the papacy. In 1157 Cardinal Bandinelli, papal legate to the diet of Besancon which hoped to iron out the difficulties between pope and Holy Roman Emperor, reminded the Emperor Frederick and his German barons that it was the vicar of Christ who had given him the signal favour of the crown. At this there was a howl of outrage, but Bandinelli, a prelate of steel and a later pope, rose to the occasion. 'From whom then', he demanded, 'does the emperor hold the empire if not from the pope?'

In 1154 Pope Anastasius IV died in Rome, an old man whose illness had prevented him making any impression on history, the successor to the Cistercian Eugenius III. He died as the armies of the Emperor Frederick Barbarossa were about to be launched on Italy and Rome in an attempt to combine the ecclesiastical and civil jurisdictions under one convenient crown. The dying pope had recalled to Rome his legate in Scandinavia as the most likely antidote to the turbulence about to be unleashed. The legate's name was Nicholas Cardinal Breakspear.[1]

Born in England, Breakspear received some of his education in an Irish monastery in Germany. He entered the Cistercian Order where his scholastic achievements coupled with a facility in organisation and management enabled him to rise to the position of abbot of St Rufus at Avignon, later to be consecrated bishop and then to be seconded to the points of ecclesiastical combat in Europe. His record as an intrepid reformer had been known to his Cistercian colleague, then Pope Eugenius. He had called him from the cloister to initiate long-called-for reforms in the Church of Scandinavia. There, as in Ireland, there were thorny problems, and the most serious in the Church institutions. The handsome, pious and austere Breakspear was outstandingly successful. He composed a catechism for the Norse in the vernacular. He was created cardinal of Albano and became popularly known as 'the good cardinal' or 'the apostle of the north'.

Breakspear's return to the Eternal City occurred at the moment of Pope Anastasius' death and as the menace from the German emperor grew close. At the resulting conclave he found himself elected pope, the first and only pope of English birth. He took the name Adrian IV. He made his mark on history in many ways. No pope effected Ireland so dramatically as Adrian. Indeed, a brief consideration of his background, talents and record implies that little else than a leaning towards the Normans or the French, with a horror of disorder or laxities, could be expected of him. Now no order in Irish history would hold as much influence as the Cistercians.

What would a man like Adrian imagine the Ireland of Diarmait Mac Murchada to be? A stern celibate, he would regard Brehon society as one where the compounding of sins had accumulated into an immoral mountain. He would estimate that this caravan of sin had been travelling for hundreds of years. If there was one item of mitigation, it was that Irish society did not knowingly commit outrage. If, however, the Irish acted in defiance of the known Christian message relayed by those empowered to deliver it, then the Irish nation was anathema.

The new pope showed his grasp of reality when faced with his first hurdle at Rome. The issue at stake was his sovereignty, or proper authority, challenged firstly by the senate of Rome. He threatened to put the city under interdict. The prospect of the withdrawal of recourse to God, of the sacrament of penance, of baptism, the Eucharist and the last sacraments was too appalling to contemplate and the revolt evaporated, with its chief protagonist, Arnold de Brescia, in flight.

But the armies of the Holy Roman Emperor Frederick grew nearer. The pope decided on a direct confrontation with the emperor. They met outside Rome. Frederick, consolidated by his armed might, faced Adrian, who had nothing but a proud bearing and a retinue of apprehensive cardinals. At close quarters the pope turned his back on the emperor until the prescribed act of obeisance had been made. That was the holding by the emperor of the pope's stirrup while he dismounted from his horse. It took the emperor two days to make the gesture. The day was won, the point was made and, in exchange, it was agreed that Frederick should now be crowned Holy Roman Emperor by the pope inside the walls of Rome. This, then, was the record of Adrian IV in the first year of his pontificate. Despite his grasp of contemporary affairs he nevertheless once bemoaned his office: 'I wish I had never left England; or had lived out my life quietly in the cloisters of St Rufus; but I dared not refuse the Lord's bidding ... He has put me between the hammer and the anvil.'

By one of history's coincidences Henry II, king of England, duke of Normandy and Aquitaine, count of Anjou, Maines and Brittany, had been crowned at Westminister at the same time as Adrian had been crowned pope. Henry was the son of the count of Anjou, in the north of France, but he owed his position as king of England to the fact that his mother was a granddaughter of William the Conqueror. At the time of his coronation he was twenty-two years old, when Diarmait Mac Murchada was forty-four.

Just as Mac Murchada was aware of Norman expansion, Henry and his court were aware of the Irish situation, religious and military. Henry knew of the wealth of Ireland, of the fish-laden rivers and, like the Norse, he knew of that vital raw material, timber, especially oak. He knew of the fertility of the soil, and of the richly endowed repositories of Celtic civilisation, the monasteries. He also knew of what churchmen regarded as religious and moral abnormalities. Plans for the invasion of Ireland and its annexation were made. The man who could threaten the Holy Roman Emperor with deposition, was the man whose blessing and goodwill were worth more than armies. And that man by blessed fortune was pope, Cistercian, and of Henry's realm and culture.

And so we meet another man,[2] a disciple of Bernard of Clairveaux, and a chronicler himself, who lived to see Henry's designs furthered. His name was John of Salisbury. He, too, was a monk and the man chosen by Henry II as his ambassador to the Holy See with the mission of obtaining the papal fiat for the proposed conquest of Ireland. He was later, as bishop of Chartres in France, to record this claim:

At my solicitation he (Pope Adrian) gave and granted Ireland to Henry II, the illustrious king of England, to hold by hereditary right, as his (the pope's) letter which to this day testifies.

John of Salisbury urged the Holy Father to approve the design which Henry II had of conquering Ireland, promising to reform the 'enormous disorders and unchristian practices in that island, and to enforce the payment of Peter's Pence to the pope from every house.' Adrian knew of the irregularities directly from Irish ecclesiastical sources, particularly from Gilla Críst, bishop of Lismore and papal legate to the Irish nation.[3]

The pope, in the belief that he had the power to so dispose of Ireland no less than any other kingdom in Christendom, granted the concession, and accepted the promise of Peter's Pence and reformation. He thereupon issued the Papal Bull 'Laudabilitur' and presented it to John of Salisbury for his master Henry.

Adrian, bishop, servant of the servants of God, to our well beloved son in Christ, the illustrious king of the English, health and apostolical benediction.[4]

Since you intimate to us, well beloved son in Christ, that you wish to enter the island of Hibernia to subject that people to laws and root out the nurseries of vice from it, and are willing to pay from each house one denarius annually assess to blessed Peter, and to preserve the rights of the Church of that land unimpaired and inviolate, so we, seconding your pious and laudable desire with the favour it deserves, and according to your request a benignant assent, are pleased and willing that to extend the bounds of the Church and for preventing the re-growth of vice (recursu) and for amending morals and sowing the seeds of virtue and for the advancement of the Christian religion, you shall enter that island and do therein what tends to the honour of God and the salvation of the people.

This dispensation takes us back to the time of Constantine the Great, emperor of Rome, and the reigning pontiff, Pope Sylvester. It refers to a claim on the part of the pope in addition to his spiritual power to be the temporal owner of the western empire from the Adriatic to St George's Channel. The pope claimed the disposition of islands. The donation of Constantine, as it was called, was universally accepted by orthodox and jurists as genuine. It is small consolation to anyone today to realise that the document so heavily relied upon for centuries by several popes and jurists is now known to be a forgery manufactured in the first half of the eighth century. It was claimed to be spurious by Laurentius Valla in the fifteenth century.

The Holy Father presented Henry with something else which by the known usage of the day was more significant than the Papal Bull. John of Salisbury tells us:

> *The Holy Father also sent by me a ring of gold with the best of emeralds set therein, wherewith the investiture might be made for Henry's governorship of Ireland and that same ring was ordered to be, and is still, in the public treasury of the king (at Winchester). If I were to state in detail its varied excellence, this one topic would supply matter for a volume.*

And so the plan was devised for the conquest of Ireland by the Norman armies, professional soldiers with not only the tradition of a century's conquest and overseas invasion but better armour, better weapons, and much more varied battle tactics than either Norse or Irish in Ireland used.

Then came the Michaelmas day of 1155 with the grand council of England at Winchester. The major enterprise for consideration and decision was the invasion of Ireland. Prior to this it had been proposed that the kingship of Ireland be bestowed on Henry's brother, William. But the invasion was opposed at the council by Henry's mother, the Empress Mathilda, and the Saxon representatives. It was decisive. The great adventure was postponed, and both the Papal Bull of Adrian and the emerald ring were sent to rest in the vaults of Winchester.

ELEVEN

Death of a King

1156, the year after Mathilda had vetoed the invasion of Ireland passed without major political eruption. But the long life of Toirdelbach Ua Conchobair, former high king and king of Connaught, was drawing to a close. Connaught watched as the problem of finding a successor to fill his shadow grew close. From Mac Murchada's point of view the anxiety was that Connaught might throw up another lion and that the cushion of restraint imposed upon it might once again be ruptured.

On 20 May, after one of the most ferociously arctic winters in Irish history, Toirdelbach Ua Conchobair breathed his last. An obituary worthy of a pontiff or Holy Roman Emperor was composed for the most eminent Ua Conchobair who ever lived.

The Augustus of the west of Europe, flood of glory and princeliness and veneration for churches and clerics, head of the prosperity and wealth of the world, one who so long as he was alive never lost a battle or a hard conflict, the one man coming from the blood of Adam's children whose mercy and bounty, charity and generosity, were best.[1]

He was interred at the high altar of Ciarán at Clonmacnois. The legacy he left to the Church for his soul's rest was considerable:

Five hundred and forty ounces of gold and forty marks of silver, and all the other valuables he had, both goblets and precious stones, both steeds and cattle, cloths, chess, and backgammon, bows and quivers, sling and arms. And he himself gave directions how each individual church's share should be given to it according to its rank.[2]

The man elected to succeed Toirdelbach was his son, Ruaidrí. Ruaidrí's first contribution to stability was the imprisonment of three of his brothers and the blinding of the eldest and most accomplished. His title to the succession was never after questioned. Ua Briain of Munster gave him hostages and so also did Tigernán Ua Ruairc of Bréifne, whose wounds had been well licked.[3] Ua Briain's gesture can be understood because the terrible losses at the battle of Móin Mór had left him petrified of losing his independence. Ua Ruairc's throw of the dice was much more precarious, for he lay between Ua Conchobair and the Mac Lochlainn-Mac Murchada axis which was well nigh impregnable.

Diarmait involved himself irredeemably in the fortunes of Mac Lochlainn.[4] His experiences had taught him that he had no other choice and to him the alliance appeared to be without challenge. With this support Mac Lochlainn was now the strongest king in Ireland by a considerable lead. In return for Mac Murchada's substantial contribution, he confirmed Mac Murchada once more in the possession of the kingdom of Leinster and the Norse. Scandal or no scandal, rape or abduction, Mac Murchada was firmly reigning.

At the same time there were those neither happy with Mac Murchada nor agreeable to recognising Mac Lochlainn as high king. These were the persistently hostile rulers of Osraige, the enemies of Uí Chennselaig and the killers of Diarmait's son, Donnchad. Mac Lochlainn himself descended upon Osraige, hitherto independent of the kings of Leinster and made it a dependency of Leinster.[5] Soon after this Mac Murchada moved without compunction to alter the ruling regime in Osraige. He expelled Cerball Mac Gilla Pátraic and handed over his territory once more to Donnchad Mac Gilla Pátraic. Cerball was never permitted to return. Donnchad, an amiable man, thus became again king of all Osraige except the Ua Cáellaide portion. He continued in control and is best remembered as the founder of the Cistercian abbey of Jerpoint in 1158. He died in 1162 and was succeeded by his nephew Domnall,[6] a man who was to prove another bitter antagonist to Diarmait Mac Murchada.

In 1156 a considerable shock undermined Mac Murchada's power. It was the unexpected death of Meath's ruler, Máel Sechlainn Ua Máel Sechlainn, Derbforgaill's brother.[7] He had reigned for a mere two years over his united territory. His death was as violent as it was abrupt: he was poisoned and died in agony at Durrow. The succession in this vital kingdom now lay between his two sons, Diarmait and Donnchad. A Mac Lochlainn-orientated ruler was of importance to the continued stability of the Mac Lochlainn-Mac Murchada axis. Mac Murchada and Mac Lochlainn wanted Donnchad to be made king but the electors of Meath preferred Diarmait Ua Máel Sechlainn.

A violent dispute at once raged between the two Ua Máel Sechlainns, Diarmait and his brother Donnchad, over the kingdom of Meath.[8] Donnchad Ua Máel Sechlainn was eventually nominated king of Meath by Mac Lochlainn with Mac Murchada's support. Forced upon the Meathmen, he was instantly deposed. A militant player in his deposition was not only his brother, Diarmait, but the phoenix Tigernán Ua Ruairc. Mac Murchada with his Uí Chennselaig men and a contingent from the Norse of Dublin found no difficulty in defeating Ua Ruairc and Diarmait Ua Máel Sechlainn. The immediate result was that Donnchad Ua Máel Sechlainn was restored to power. There was, however, a repeated and even costlier omission. Mac Murchada did not believe that there was any urgency in the molesting or mutilation of Ua Ruairc. It was an omission that would ultimately break him.

Ruaidrí Ua Conchobair was bound, inevitably, to challenge the power and jurisdiction of the high king Mac Lochlainn. If age had dampened the edge of the old Ua Conchobair, the reverse was true for the young blooded Ruaidrí. But Mac Lochlainn had too much of a head start. One property favoured Ruaidrí: his age. He would outlive Mac Lochlainn provided an assassin was kept away. Mac Murchada knew this too, and yet backed Mac Lochlainn. Mac Murchada knew that his attempt at major power could only come, and must come, on the decrease of Mac Lochainn's personal fortunes. It was through this narrow gap, providing that alliances and the fates were propitious that the opportunity would lie. Until that gap appeared the course of action would be the continued build up of prestige, wealth and power in Leinster.

The challenge from Ruaidrí Ua Conchobair to the high king Mac Lochlainn became more strident. There was, however, no head-on collision at the beginning of Ruaidrí's reign. What happened was a series of demonstrations of strength, attempts by one party to undermine the other. As in Meath, an Ua Conchobair nomination or subking would be deposed by Mac Murchada and Mac Lochlainn, with the inevitable punitive sweep in its trail. Similarly, where possible Ua Conchobair tried to solidify his own sphere of influence. This type of raid and counter-raid went on until 1159. In this year a rejuvenated Tigernán Ua Ruairc threw in his lot unconditionally with Ruaidrí Ua Conchobair. Mac Lochlainn now had had enough shadow boxing. His forces met the full Ua Conchobair advance which consisted of six battalions of Connaught with Ua Ruairc, and two Munster battalions, at Ardee. The Connaught and Ua Ruairc battalions were overthrown, but the two Munster battalions 'were dreadfully slaughtered'.

This bloody victory reasserted Mac Lochlainn's impregnable position as high king. In order to demonstrate who held the power in the country, if indeed further proof were necessary, Mac Lochlainn was joined by Diarmait Mac Murchada's army of Leinstermen and Norse in a punitive sweep into Connaught, Bréifne and Meath where their appointed king Donnchad Ua Máel Sechlainn was not relished.[9] In 1161 Ruaidrí accepted the inevitable publicly. He gave hostages to Muirchertach Mac Lochlainn. Mac Lochlainn had reached the pinnacle of his career, the goal of every Irish monarch. He was high king 'without opposition'.

In the kingdom of Meath, however, another unexpected coup fermented. The ruler favoured by Mac Murchada and Mac Lochlainn, Donnchad Ua Máel Sechlainn, was killed by a minor chieftain, the lord of Delbna Mór. Donnchad Ua Máel Sechlainn was eliminated 'because of the grudges against him, and through his own fault'. With no opposition from then on, Donnchad's brother Diarmait Ua Máel Sechlainn, ruled Meath unchallenged; and, while doing so, fertilised his grudge against Mac Murchada.

And Tigernán Ua Ruairc still lived without mutilation.

TWELVE

'The Man who is not Strong ...'

It cannot be said about Mac Murchada that at one particular point in his life he went wrong, or started to go wrong. These changes in his course were imperceptible at the time and apparent as strategies of genius or disaster only in hindsight as the consequences of these moves were evaluated.

Mac Murchada was a cunning man.[1] It was bred in him. The choice of the ruling family to which he was sent as a foster son made sure of that, for his foster parents, the Ua Cáellaide, were the Achilles' heel of enemy Osraige, the enemies of Osraige's predominant king, and the custodians of the territory between Uí Chennselaig and Norse Waterford. There is an Irish proverb which runs *An te nac bhfuil laidir, ni folair do bheith glic,* ('It is essential for the man who is not strong to be cunning'). It might have been the legend on the Mac Murchada coat of arms. He ran with the hare and hunted with the hounds. Despite indifference to the ecclesiastical moral code, he was a generous benefactor of the Church.

He influenced the appointment of abbots and bishops. He had seen his second foster brother, Dungal Ua Cáellaide, raised to the rank of bishop and appointed to rule over the western portion of Uí Chennselaig, namely, the diocese of Leighlin. He engineered unions of wedlock for his daughters only to princes of potential. He played the hand dealt to him by fate with brilliance. It must not be forgotten that, alone, he could never hope for the ultimate in power. It is conceivable that he doubted that he might ultimately be high king since no one knew better than he about the element of luck involved. But he was always building the edifice or conditions for a Mac Murchada to become high king in the future. His weakness was his ambition for the high kingship at any cost to himself or others. Despite his indifference to the Church norms, he was on excellent personal terms with the senior clerics of Ireland, and was only one among very many, clerical as well as lay, who recognised the pre-eminence of the Brehon code. Mac Murchada's early life was unreal for a sixteen year old. We have the advantage of knowing the traditions that fired his imagination.

The *Book of Leinster* is a compilation of the books, journals, poems, fables and historic sagas which comprised Diarmait Mac Murchada's tradition. The original collection is part of the rich treasure of old Irish manuscripts in Trinity College today.[2] This was compiled or transcribed in the 1100s by Aed Mac Crimthainn, Professor of Ferns and Diarmait's lector, along with Finn Ua Gormain, bishop of Kildare. It begins with the *Book of the Invasion of Ireland*, after which follows the vital record of successions of kings of Ireland and it continues with the lists of kings and obituaries of provincial and lesser kings. It includes a great many poems about the wars of the Leinstermen, the Ulstermen, and the Munstermen with the emphasis on the superiority of the Leinstermen in all matters: 'If I had seven heads I could not tell all the prowess of the Leinstermen even in a month, without seven tongues in each separate head'. Some of the poems are believed to have been written by the celebrated poet and antiquarian Dubhthach. Then there is the long narrative poem of the Boru tribute and its eventual remission, the wonderful *Meisce Uladh* or the Ulster Drunkenness. It was a regal drunkenness, a tribute to the hospitality of the king, Conchobar Mac Nessa. At one stage the poem pays tribute to one of the guests who 'from the day he took spear in his hand wounded or killed every day some man of Connaught, and never slept comfortably unless the body of a Connaught man formed his pillow'. Another volume deals with the battle of Cennabrat in Munster, with the defeat of Mac Con by Oilioll Oluim, Mac Con's subsequent flight into Scotland, his later return with a large force of Scottish and British mercenaries and the ensuing battle of Magh Macruimhe, fought between him and his uncle, Art the high king in which Art was defeated and killed.

The volumes do not all relate to deeds of conquest. There is a copy of the *Dinnsenchus*, the topographical tract compiled at Tara in 550, several poems on the geography of the known world, chronology, history and so on. There are the pedigrees and genealogies of the great dynasties and families – again with emphasis on the Leinster ones. Lastly, to balance the spirit against the sword, there is a comprehensive list of the early saints of Ireland with their pedigrees and affinities and with copious references to the exact location of their churches and abbey complexes.

This collection is an indication of the material on which Diarmait Mac Murchada's imagination was fuelled. The legends incorporated the world view and regard for the glory of conquest with the qualities of swordsmanship, ruthlessness, guile and organisation necessary for those who aspire to the acquisition of power. Mac Murchada had these qualities. What he did not ultimately possess was luck.

From the mid-1150s he was as secure as life permitted in his kingdom. Coasting with a fair wind in his back, he entered upon a decade unprecedented in Leinster for progress, trade, building, expansion, art and ecclesiastical foundation. It was a decade of stirring ecclesiastical development in which Mac Murchada's influence was felt. The Norse did not regard the Irish Church authorities with favour. The bishops of their city dioceses – Dublin, Wexford, Waterford were consecrated by the archbishop of Canterbury and were invariably Norse. In 1154 the old bishop of Ferns died and was succeeded by a young man who was to occupy the see for thirty years. His name was Seosamh Ua hAeda.[3] First styled bishop of Ferns, he was, before the decade had passed, also to be styled bishop of Wexford.[4] Mac Murchada had established 'so great a sway over the Norse as had not been known before,' and that sway was imposed from the Irish sea's merchant hub and major port of Dublin right around to the Atlantic coast.

There were vigorous steps in the Church's efforts to put everything in order. The old-time institutions of the Irish Church – the monasteries – had no common set of rules or constitution.

The monasteries were all independent but varied in severity, or, for that matter, laxity. The organisation of the Canons Regular of St Augustine was attracting many houses in the monastic system. New monasteries were founded for it, and old monasteries declared themselves for the Augustinian rule. Among the latter was one of the most interesting, a monastery dedicated to St Renduane and devoted to the care and custody of one of Europe's earliest lighthouses.[5] Situated on the point of the Hook, a snarling knife of rock that cuts into the Atlantic at the mouth of Waterford harbour, the lighthouse, which consisted of a large beacon on top of the monks' stoutly built monastery/lighthouse, had been kindled and kept blazing by the monks for hundreds of years.

Mac Murchada decided to adorn his capital with another foundation.[6] He founded the abbey of Ferns under the invocation of the Virgin Mary. The men he chose for the monastery located inside his own capital were the reforming Canons Regular following the rule of St Augustine. The wording of the foundation charter is interesting, as are the signatures of the witnesses, recording as they do the papal legate, Gilla Croist Ó Conairche, his foster brother, Dungal Ua Cáellaide, bishop of Leighlin, his own bishop, other Leinster bishops, his chancellor, his chaplain, his brother-in-law, Lorcan Ua Tuathail, abbot of Glendalough and the representative of the Norsemen, Lorquan, the son of Dubhgaill. The foundation charter in Latin has been translated into English which reads:

Charter of the foundation of the abbey of Ferns, 1158 by Diarmait Mac Murchada, king of Leinster.

To all the sons of Holy Mother Church, archbishops, bishops, abbots, earls, barons, and all others, as well clergy as laity, Diarmait, by will of God, king of Leinster, sends greetings. Be it known that I, by the counsel and advice of the principal men (of my council) have given and granted, and by this my charter have confirmed to God and the Blessed Virgin Mary (for the monastery) which I have founded at Ferns and to the canons there serving God, the following lands, namely Balisfin, Balilacussa, for one village; Borin and Roshena, and Kilbride, for two villages; the lands of Ballifislan in Forth near Wexford, the vill(age) called Munemethe in Ferneghenan, and a certain cell at Thaghmoling, being the chapel of St Mary, with all belongings, with the land of Balligery with all the fisheries and my chapel, with all the tithes and first fruits of the lordship of Uí Ceinnsellach, and a certain measure called Scaith, out of every measure called a Lagen, or gallon, in the brewing of beer made in the town of Ferns; to be held of men and my heirs by the said canons in pure and perpetual alms, for the health of my soul and my ancestors and successors.

As also the cell of Finach in Ferns, with Baliculum, and Balinafusin, and three acres close to the same cell.

I also will and firmly ordain that the said house and canons there serving God, shall have hold and possess the said lands in the aforesaid alms for me, my heirs and successors, completely in peace, fully and wholly, without paying any rent, or (rendering) any secular service, neither to bishop, king, earl nor any other man, in wood, in plain, in meadows, in pastures, and in fisheries, which belong to me and to my heirs, in waters, in mills, in roads and paths, in moors and marshes, and in all other liberties and free customs, which I and my heirs are able to grant and warrant to the said canons and their successors. I and my heirs are bound to warrant the same house in the aforesaid lands and possessions to the same canons and their successors, against all men and women. I have also conceded to them that in any elections or removals of abbots of the same house no heir of mine ought to meddle, but that he who is to be ordained should be freely constituted according to the rule of St Augustine by the consent of his convent or the major part of them, and after the election of the same, before he be created abbot by the archbishop or bishop, he shall be presented to me, or my heirs or their seneschals by reason of the lordship, that through us he may be blessed by the bishop.

Given this 21 February at Ferns, these being witness: Gilla Críst, bishop of Lismore and apostolic legate of all Ireland. Donatus, bishop of Leighlin, Josephus, bishop of Ferns, Donald, bishop of Ossory; Malachy, bishop of Kildare; Celestine, bishop of Glendalough; Lorcan, abbot of Glendalough; Florence the king's chancellor; Mark, the chaplain; Lorquan, the son of Dubhgaill; Gilla Pátraic Ua Murchada and many others.

No clearer evidence of Mac Murchada's mental agility will be found than in the last sentence of his charter to the Augustinian abbey of Ferns 'and after the election of same (the abbot) before he be created abbot by the archbishop or bishop, he shall be presented to me, or my heirs or the seneschals by reason of the lordship, that through us he may be blessed by the bishop'. Adverse developments had been catered for.

Diarmait's abbey would have one feature to make it unique. The lower portion of this tower is square up to a height of thirty feet. After that, it becomes the traditional round tower so beloved of Irish monks. Its outline and former extent indicate that it was a distinct contribution to the capital of Leinster.

Mac Murchada, a man tall of stature and a large frame, had now seen a family grow up around him. He kept them to himself. Not unnatural for a father except when one examines the twelfth century, when ruling fathers regarded their grown sons as rivals, and some growing sons as better out of the way as foster children. None of his children were sent as foster children or hostages. Mac Murchada held on to them, trained them, taught them, shared with them the prestige. He complemented the tuition of Mac Crimthainn with his own expertise. Domnall and Énna, his grown sons, never exhibited a trace of disloyalty to their father. In that age it was unusual.

Mac Murchada's wife, Mór, had presented him with two more children of promise. They named their son Conchobar and their daughter Aífe. Both of them had grown toward maturity with the best qualities of both parent's families. Diarmait's eldest son, Domnall Caemanach Mac Murchada, had himself married and had fathered Diarmait's first known grandson.

Domnall Caemanach was his father's trusted right hand who in 1161 commanded the expedition which brought the Wexford Vikings back into line following brief antagonism. It was a consolidated, well-adjusted family which prospered with Mac Murchada as the decade of the sixties saw him achieve even greater consequence than before. His daughters, Órlaith and Derbforgaill, were now almost adults. Órlaith married Domnall Mór Ua Briain, the son of Toirdelbach, the king of Thomond, with whom there had been such costly strife. It was a union loaded with significance in every respect; politics, support, prestige. Derbforgaill, his third daughter, married another man of promise, Domnall Mac Gilla Mo Cholmóc of Cuala,[7] the more remarkable in that Diarmait had had his uncle blinded. Very satisfactorily, Domnall was a man for the future. His family's ruling area ran from Inch on the northern boundary of Uí Chennselaig right up to the gates of Viking Dublin.

Mac Murchada constantly rewarded his foster father's family at this stage of his power.[8] The Ua Cáellaide maintained thereby a permanent and strong position in Osraige. After Mac Murchada's day they never again knew eminence and their memory faded. The Ua Cerbaill episcopal see of Airgailla had been filled and maintained by Diarmait's foster brother Aed Ua Cáellaide. In view of the role of the bishop, it speaks for Mac Murchada's standing with the high king Mac Lochlainn, Ua Cerbaill the ruler of Airgailla and the archbishop of Armagh, that so intimate a connection from the south should securely reign in the north. Even after twenty years in that diocese, Mac Murchada described him in the Charter to All Hallows as 'his spiritual father and confessor' and appointed him trustee of that endowment.[9]

The Norse archbishop of Dublin, Gregory, died in 1161. It was clear at that stage, for many geographical and strategic reasons, that Dublin was the city of the future. In size it was the only Irish city to compare with a major European city port, and it was the centre of the Norse Sea Empire. But the time had come when the appointment of a Scandinavian as archbishop of Dublin consecrated by Canterbury was no longer tolerable. And so the dramatic news. The new archbishop of Dublin was Lorcan Ó Tuathail, an Irishman. He was only thirty-four years of age and the abbot of Glendalough, a former hostage in Ferns, the youngest son of the ruler of Uí Muiredaig of the house of Ó Tuathail and brother of Diarmait Mac Murchada's wife and queen, Mór. At the consecration of Lorcan Ó Tuathail the triumphant celebration of ecclesiastical Ireland was manifest. He was consecrated by the archbishop of Armagh, the primate of all Ireland. One of the co-consecrators was Diarmait's bishop of Ferns, Seosamh Ua hAeda.

Diarmait's control of Dublin was made complete in 1162 after a renewed assertion of Viking independence. He was the great port's real master, although he deputised his son Énna to regulate the Norse citadel. Mac Murchada then dispensed ecclesiastical largesse. He founded the monastery of All Hallows for the Canons Regular of the Arrouasian Augustinians.[10] Today it is Trinity College, Dublin. He also granted his lands at Baldoyle (where the modern Augustinians have a house) together with its serfs, to the priory of All Hallows. The first witness to his charter is that of the first of Diarmait's race to follow his name with the title, archbishop of Dublin. Diarmait then confirmed by charter land at Killenny in Idrone to Felix, abbot of Osraige for the construction of a monastery dedicated to St Mary and St Benedict. The first witness' signature to the grant was that of Lorcan Ó Tuathail, archbishop of Dublin.

The only ripple of discontent to occur at this time was in the appointment of an abbot to succeed Lorcan in Glendalough. The abbot of Glendalough had considerably more power than its bishop. Moreover, since it was in the home ruling area of the Ó Tuathail's it was an Ó Tuathail nominee who was invariably elected. Lorcan Ó Tuathail proposed the appointment of his own nephew to succeed him as abbot. Diarmait Mac Murchada was opposed to this. He nominated his own reliable choice, Benignus, to succeed and achieved abbatial honours in Glendalough.

Mac Murchada's greatest hour for national recognition and the benediction of the Church was undoubtedly when he sponsored, attended and protected the synod in 1162.[11] Held at Clane on the Liffey, it convened the clergy of all Ireland. It was presided over by Gilla Maic Liac, archbishop of Armagh, and attended by twenty-six bishops, including the pope's representative, Gilla Críst Ua Connairche. The synod listed on its agenda the necessity of uniformity of doctrine and the primacy of Armagh. It was decreed that no one could be a professor to any church in the country unless he was an alumnus of Armagh. Though late in the day, the enactments of the synod of Clane were determined milestones passed on the road to what Pope Adrian would describe as the reforming of disorders and unchristian practices. With decrees against concubinage and unnatural unions enacted at the previous synod of Kells, there was sufficient resolution on paper to satisfy the most scrupulous prelate at the Lateran, provided the precepts were observed.

A contributory factor to Mac Murchada's eminence at this time was that, in comparison with the other rulers, he was relatively peaceful. Whether he held his peace from weakness, opportunism or attempted consolidation is a matter for debate. The fact was that from 1160 the Ua Conchobair of Connaught military activities resumed.[12] Hostages were extracted from the Ua Briains, the Ua Máel Sechlainns, the Mac Fáeláins and the Ua Fáilge. Continual efforts were made to loosen the last two from Mac Murchada's grip. Mac Lochlainn had to renew violent pressure on Ua Conchobair and was forced once more, in 1161, to extract further hostages from him. The need for patronage of a synod was, however, apparent. The appearance of Mac Murchada as its protector was a mark of his rehabilitation. The synod did embark on an extra-ecclesiastical course. 'They confirmed the election of certain kings with their regulations.'

Diarmait Mac Murchada was consolidated in power and administration in Dublin, Leinster and Uí Chennselaig by 1162, a situation which seemed as secure as its potential was obvious. He made and unmade regimes in dependent enclaves with no seeming difficulty. In the early years of the decade he was only involved in strife overseas. Dublin and Leinster people became drawn into warfare in Scotland and its western isles. War was raised between the Norse king of the Hebrides and Cinn Tir with the men of Scotland. A great fleet of swift war vessels assembled in Dublin and skimmed the waves to assist their Norse brothers. They limped home with heavy losses, after the harsh winter storms of 1164.

It was the following year, 1165, that Henry II, king of the Normans renewed contact with Diarmait Mac Murchada. The major cities of trade and intimate contact with Leinster and Dublin were Bristol and Chester. Both were strongholds of support for Henry II when his own struggle for power was intense. The normal interchange of mercenaries on both sides of the Irish Sea was a lucrative tradition from the time of Diarmait's greatest predecessor, Diarmait Mac Maél na mBó.[13] Henry was under assault when the rulers of Wales made war on the French, as the Welsh chronicle, Brut y Tywsogion, called the Normans. Henry was in such trouble that his hard-won power was being systematically undermined. The angry Welsh campaign was not contained in 1164 and Henry engaged the armed assistance of Diarmait Mac Murchada early in 1165.

The common contact and friend who advanced the bond between Diarmait and Henry was the Portreeve of Bristol, Robert FitzHarding. Few diplomats have been possessed of such a confluence of power as FitzHarding in that decade. Henry procured by arrangement a combined fleet of Diarmait's Leinstermen and Norse. The force was assembled and launched from Leinster. On his side across the English border, Henry marched to overwhelm the Welsh from the rear. His springboard was his own stronghold at Chester. The threat to the Norman monarch dissolved and Henry breathed easily once more. Henry was in Diarmait Mac Murchada's debt, although in the course of affairs in the Irish Sea province few decades progressed without either side engaging hired swords swiftly delivered in ships manned by the Norse.

At the same time as these seaborne adventures occupied Mac Murchada's mind there was internecine strife in Thomond. Toirdelbach Ua Briain, the battered king of Thomond, was still at arms. They had overwhelmed the Mac Carthaigs again and with them the ruler of Ormond whom they blinded. In the opinion of his son Muirchertach however, Toirdelbach had reigned and possibly lived for too long. Muirchertach himself raised revolt against his own father.[14] Toirdelbach was banished, but there was now a contact in Thomond to see that at least the old man could find a haven of comfort. Diarmait Mac Murchada's daughter, Órlaith, was married to Domnall Mór Ua Briain, later king. The deposed Toirdelbach sought refuge in Uí Chennselaigh where Diarmait Mac Murchada offered the old patriarch and one-time enemy from the battle of Moin Mór, hospitality and help.[15]

Nevertheless the decade of progress which started in Ferns ended in the flames of Gaelic Leinster's capital. Fire as a result of war was always to be expected, but in the noonday of peace a major fire was far from anticipated by the occupants of Ferns. The town, apart from the fortress, abbey, cathedral and church, was made up of dwellings constructed of timber for the most part. Marl bricks and fortified mud-walls with thatch and wickerwork provided variations, but nevertheless the whole thing cried fire hazard. In 1165 that hazard was realised.[16] At the extreme end of the town a fire in a dwelling spread to the roof. Within seconds the house was a furnace. The alarm raised the population, but as neighbours ran to help the gutted house the fire fanned by the breeze turned into a conflagration. In a few minutes Ferns was transformed into a gale of fire, sparks, smoke and heat. Mac Murchada saw his pleasant town, with the exception of the castle, monastery, cathedral and churches, devoured. The severity of the damage is explained by the nature of the buildings and also demonstrates why towns burnt down so frequently, as reported by annalists. Mac Murchada decided to rebuild Ferns. The raw materials of construction were near at hand and this enabled rapid reconstruction. Mac Murchada spurred his people to renewal from the ashes. When the debris was cleared, the laborious task was commenced and inside a year a new Ferns had been built.

But it was a rebuilding that was to make a larger and more ferocious fire in the fateful year ahead. For although there was no evidence that humiliation was at hand, the golden years of Diarmait Mac Murchada were at an end, and the raiment of power and prestige which clothed his bulk was soon to be exchanged for the rags of the beggar.

THIRTEEN

Disaster

Mac Lochlainn, king of Ireland, had only one threat to maintaining supremacy in the north. Eochaid Mac Duinn Sléibe and his people were reluctant accomplices to the strongest ruler in Ireland. At the same time as the great fire in Ferns this reluctance came to a head and the people of Ulster turned against Mac Lochlainn.[1]

Mac Lochlainn's response was one of ruthless severity, his course of action so dire in its long execution and consequences that one is inclined to doubt the high king's sanity. The strongest soldier in Ireland, the ruling high king with no equal, entered this territory with a large army, ravished the land and crops, and killed 'a countless number of the inhabitants'. Their king, Mac Duinn Sléibe, was expelled, and the soldiers of the high king withdrew, sated. When the initial dismay had worn off Airgialla's king, Ua Cerbaill, approached the high king and impressed upon him the importance of restoring Mac Duinn Sléibe with full rights. Ua Cerbaill was deeply interested in this, for he was the foster father of Mac Duinn Sléibe. This then was finally and grudgingly agreed upon. However, as pledges for his loyalty Mac Duinn Sléibe was compelled to give Mac Lochlainn as hostage a son of every chieftain in Ulster – and Mac Duinn Sléibe's own daughter to the high king personally. That was in 1165.

The next spring, with what can only be described as one of the most extraordinary examples of vindictiveness in Irish history, Mac Lochlainn put to death his hostages, Mac Duinn Sléibe's daughter and the sons of ruling potential of the principal chieftains in Ulster. Finally he incapacitated the wretched Mac Duinn Sléibe by blinding him 'against the guarantees of Ua Cerbaill, the king of Airgialla, after dishonouring the comarb of St Patrick, and the staff of Jesus, and the comarb of Columba, and the gospel of St Martin and many clergy ...'[2] The support of Airgialla and Ulster evaporated immediately and with total effect from the Mac Lochlainn alliance. The fabric of strength Mac Murchada and Mac Lochlainn had fortified in war, made durable in peace and in which they placed future hope, crashed in ruins.

Before Mac Murchada had time to assess the consequences of Mac Lochlainn's outrage or to take steps to heal the breach, Ruairdrí Ua Conchobair of Connaught and Tigernán Ua Ruairc of Bréifne, with their combined forces, were on his throat.[3] Piece by piece the plan to bring about Mac Murchada's total reduction was accomplished. First the Ua Conchobair army with the gleeful Ua Ruairc marched through Meath where they collected hostages from Diarmait Ua Máel Sechlainn. They then made for Dublin where the Norsemen not only submitted but made an alliance with Ua Conchobair. And inside Dublin city, for the first time, Ruaidrí Ua Conchobair was inaugurated high king of Ireland 'as honourably as any king of the Gael was ever inaugurated.'[4] The honour cost Ruaidrí 4,000 cows paid to the Norse of Dublin, evidence, if needed, of that city's importance.[5]

With Dublin and Meath gone to Ruaidrí, there was no hope for Mac Murchada against the oncoming tide.[6] When Ua Conchobair procured the submission of Ua Cerbaill of Airgialla at Mellifont, victory was out of the question for Mac Murchada. But what about his sub-kings? Mac Murchada, with fever in his blood and the defence of the glory that had been built up with so much pain and patience over several decades uppermost in his mind, urged his sub-kings to stay the flood of enemies. Mac Murchada realised that if they could reach stalemate there would be a mutual withdrawal as had happened so often in the past and all would be well. But no. There was no one to stand by him. No one. Not even the family his daughter had entered, the Mac Gilla Mo Cholmóc. As soon as Ruaidrí's forces reached Uí Fáeláin, the ruler submitted and entered Ruaidrí's confederation. So too with Uí Failge. None of their rulers had any reason to be grateful to Mac Murchada for anything unless it was that he spared them the honour of ruling

Leinster. The Ua Tuathail? No! Osraige? Their new Mac Gilla Pátraic king would revel in mutilating him.

Ruadri cemented the new alliance he raised against the Mac Murchada–Mac Lochlainn grouping when he bestowed 240 cows on Ua Cerbaill of Airgialla on receiving his submission and gave a similar number of cows to Ua Fáeláin, the Uí Failge, and to Osraige. Offerings in exchange for hostages were so considerable that no ruler could avoid the Ua Conchobair invitation. And a very moderate invitation was all that was required.

Mac Murchada was now at the point of desperation. Encountering desertions both predictable and unexpected, he was faced with another doubt. The defensive blanket of Ferns was the *Dubh-tír*, a mat of trees and vegetation. The ruler who controlled that wall inside Mac Murchada's Uí Chennselaig was Murchad Ua Brain. The loyalty of any subordinate chieftain by this stage could no longer be assumed. Mac Murchada concluded that this man must be investigated for his reliance despite his previous unbending loyalty.[7] An emissary was dispatched to Ua Brain, in the robes of an Augustinian friar from Ferns. The result brought confirmation of his doubt. Murchad Ua Brain repudiated, insulted and deserted Diarmait Mac Murchada[8].

The king of Leinster was now beyond the point of desperation. All was gone. He had no army save his own Uí Chennselaig men between him and the vengeance of Ua Conchobair and Ua Ruairc. No Norsemen either. No generals of equal ability to confer with or mastermind a battle plan. On the contrary, those who knew his mind were organised against him, essaying his destruction. No Munstermen, no Waterford or Wexford men to fortify him. There was nothing to defend the work and achievement of a lifetime, no inheritance of honour, promise or potential to bequeath to his sons. Mac Murchada decided on a last stand for victory or destruction, for he had no illusions if Ua Ruairc were the eventual victor.

He chose the battlefield. Since Ua Brain's desertion, the secrets and protection of the *Dubhtír* were lost. He had to move his defences out beyond the barrier of the Blackstairs mountains. Fid

Dorcha in modern county Carlow near Clonegal was selected.[9] It was a thick dark wood never before used as a defensive position and thus it provided the only surprise which Diarmait had up his sleeve. It lay across the gateway to the passes into his capital, the route his enemies must take if they were to avoid the mountains. It was as thick as a crow's nest. His leaders alongside him were his brother, Murchad, and his son, Domnall Cáemánach Mac Murchada. As he waited the arrival of his exultant enemies, there was a further gnawing fear. Were the Norsemen of Wexford going to attack him from the rear? As the man of fifty-six years of age waited with blinking eyes, he must have scarce believed the extent to which he was reduced.

The battle was lost before it was begun. Although his men fought to preserve the sun in which they had long bathed, the pass was forced by the overwhelming numbers of his foes, Irish and Norse, and Diarmait Mac Donnchada Mac Murchada, king of Leinster and the Norse, found himself in the autumn of his vigour with 'no glory except the corpses of the men of Uí Chennselaig.'[10]

The high king did not ravage Uí Chennselaig. The example of what Mac Lochlainn had done was fresh before the minds of all. Even in defeat, Mac Murchada still had the aura of prestige. Nor was Ua Ruairc allowed to molest him. Nevertheless Diarmait himself had forestalled pillage on the grand scale by ordering Ferns to be burnt once more to the ground.

Ua Conchobair's terms were harsh but not as harsh as they might have been. He demanded and obtained Mac Murchada's submission, along with four hostages of genuine importance. He withdrew recognition of Mac Murchada as king of Leinster and the Norse and left him king of his original, core hereditary area. But Diarmait Mac Murchada was left alone, unharmed and independent. With seals set to this arrangement, Ruaidrí Ua Conchobair withdrew in triumph to his wild and beautiful kingdom of Connaught.

It is difficult to understand why he withdrew without rectifying a long standing omission. Mac Murchada had never paid the honour price to Ua Ruairc for his wife, Derbforgaill. It was not paid on this occasion either; but she was not forgotten. The bitter hatred of Diarmait Mac Murchada and Tigernán Ua Ruairc thrived because of her, surmounted deaths, defeats and destruction, while she showed gratifying contrition as she eased toward her sixties.

FOURTEEN

The Great Deed Done in Ireland

When Mac Murchada's defeat and subjugation were accomplished, the victorious forces wended their way home, but he was not too paralysed for instant local retribution. The hostages he had of Osraige and Ua Fáeláin, including one of Ua Fáeláin's sons, were dispatched, and, at his instigation, Mac Gilla Mo Cholmóc, the ruler of his daughter's new homeland, was assassinated.[1] The man who dispatched Mo Cholmoc was Diarmait's first cousin, Ua Bráenáin of Kilteel and Uí Máel Ruba. The effect of that deed was the election of Diarmait's son-in-law to succeed as the Mac Gilla Mo Cholmóc, king of what assuredly was the area of maximum growth in Ireland, Cuala. While Mac Murchada was showing defiance in his ruin, his one time ally, the former high king Mac Lochlainn, was being hunted from bog to bog as if he were vermin.[2]

His own family had turned against Mac Lochlainn, his Church had disavowed him. The odds looked right to Tigernán Ua Ruairc, and when Mac Lochlainn's own people invited him and Ua Cerbaill to join them in administering the *coup de grace,* there was no more willing accomplice. Mac Lochlainn was run to ground in the Fews of Armagh, called *Leitir Luin,* and slaughtered.[3] *The Annals of Ulster* could not conceal the awe at what had come to pass:

> *A great marvel and wonderful deed was then done: to wit, the king of Ireland to fall without battle, without contest, after his dishonouring the successor of Patrick, the staff of Jesus, and the successor of Columcille, and the gospel of St Martin and many clergy besides.*

To Mac Murchada's mind, there was now added the abject misery of mighty Mac Lochlainn's end, notwithstanding the ruthlessness of his last days. As for Ua Ruairc, he had returned from the grave's edge and was improving with every hour. But his honour had not been satisfied. Mac Murchada must be humiliated and destroyed, or blinded perhaps. Too late for castration. But something appropriate to his indiscretions would be just. Ua Ruairc realised that Mac Murchada was still, man for man, his equal. He would therefore seek out other interested parties to join in one last expedition into Uí Chennselaig.

There were interested parties anxious to 'take vengeance on Mac Murchada for the wife of Ua Ruairc': the Dublin Norsemen, Meath's Diarmait Ua Máel Sechlainn, Derbforgaill's nephew; the families of north Leinster, and there was Osraige and its king Mac Gilla Pátraic. The organisation of this gathering against Mac Murchada gave Ua Ruairc considerable satisfaction. It injected terror in Diarmait Mac Murchada.

What could be expected from the general of this expedition, Tigernán Ua Ruairc? Resistance before overwhelming numbers would be futile. Penetration to Uí Chennselaig and Ferns would be inevitable, despite a final stand. Fear saturated the former king of Leinster and the Norse.

It was at this point that the mental powers of Diarmait Mac Murchada were at their zenith. The course he chose to embark upon in the nightmare he was living is a determined example of survival despite all being lost. Mac Murchada decided that he would not be reduced. He would not surrender and he would not submit. He decided that he would do two things: sail to Bristol for a conference with the portreeve, Robert FitzHarding, and confer with the papal legate to Ireland, Gilla Críst Ua Connairche, bishop of Lismore.

In the uncertainty and real danger of the venture, Diarmait arranged with his Uí Chennselaig administrators and family that Murchad, his brother, should take over as ruler of Uí Chennselaig in his absence. He left behind him his family, including his trusted soldier son, Domnall Cáemánach Mac Murchada, his younger sons Énna, and Conchobar who was little more mature than his own grandson. He took with him his trusted secretary and adviser,

Maurice Ó Regan, and sped with as much security as could be provided through the ruling area of his foster brother, Ua Cáellaide, in the south of Osraige, to Lismore on the Blackwater river. There it is certain that he held a discussion with the thoroughly informed papal legate, Gilla Críst. Diarmait then put out into the Atlantic from Corcoran on the beach of Imokilly at the mouth of the Blackwater river.[4] It was the first day of August in 1166. He was Bristol bound. On board with him was a significant dynasty member, Amláib Ua Ceinnéidigh, and more than sixty-three hands.

In a period when most tributes paid to rulers were in obituaries, and when unsolicited testimonials for anyone, particularly the fallen, are non-existent, the hastily written tribute to Diarmait on the margin of one of the *Book of Leinster's* pages is more eloquent of his character and the esteem in which he was held than anything else recorded.

Oh Mary! Mary! It is a great deed that has been done in Ireland on this day, the Kalends of August; Diarmait Mac Donnchada Mac Murchada, king of Leinster and the foreigners to have been banished by the men of Ireland over the sea eastwards. Alas, Alas, O Lord! What will I do?

The fury of Ua Ruairc on finding his quarry gone and without trace was suitable to the occasion.[5] His warriors had no difficulty in penetrating to Ferns. Since the king had gone, they set upon the king's castle and his fortifications. His castle was demolished, the fortifications levelled and even the wooden balustrade torn down and burnt. The victorious then annexed the portion of northern Uí Chennselaig next to Osraige, and confirmed Diarmait's brother, Murchad, as king of Uí Chennselaig.[6] If by doing this they thought they were certain of a loyal puppet and a family feud, they grievously underestimated the loyalty of the Mac Murchadas. Murchad carried out his role with efficiency, sparing his family all turbulence until the hoped for return of Diarmait with reinforcements.

Nevertheless there was one family tragedy. Diarmait's son

Énna was taken hostage by his neighbouring enemy, Mac Gilla Pátraic of Osraige. Énna's talents and potential had already come to widespread attention and he was regarded in the Norse ports as well as Leinster as *ríghdamhna* or of ruling prospects. He was now at the mercy of a fierce rival. A further crop of hostages was sent to the high king Ruaidrí Ua Conchobair and the expedition withdrew, minus again the honour price to the husband of Derbforgaill by Diarmait Mac Murchada. But Ruaidrí Ua Conchobair was undisputed and acknowledged high king of Ireland without a rival on the scene, as far as he or anyone else could ascertain.

FIFTEEN

The Vital Link in Bristol

Robert FitzHarding is one of the most interesting figures in Anglo-Irish history, a man not one whit the less important because his role and distinction have never been emphasised.[1] He was descended from the kings of Denmark. He had the unique distinction of being at once a personal family friend of both Henry II and Diarmait Mac Murchada.

When Diarmait Mac Murchada's ship landed in Bristol, the former king of Leinster and the Norse made straight for the abode of Robert FitzHarding. This was situated near the waterfront in the priory of the reforming Canons Regular of St Augustine. His immediate visit to FitzHarding, and to FitzHarding's residence has been treated casually by some historians. Why did Mac Murchada trip as if by force of habit to the place of residence of FitzHarding? What was the reason for their friendship? That takes us back to his great-grandfather, Diarmait Mac Máel na mBó, the first and only Uí Chennselaig ruler to be regarded king of Ireland.[2]

The world knows the story of William the Conqueror and of Harold who was killed by the Norman invaders while leading the English in 1066. Before this event, however, the causes of the Norman invasion of England were being fermented. As early as 1051, Harold's family was the most formidable obstacle to Norman ambition and they had to fly from their land before the Norman sympathiser, King Edward the Confessor. Harold and his brothers fled to Bristol and from there took ship to Dublin. They were received by Diarmait's great-grandfather, Diarmait Mac Máel na mBó, who helped them and gave them both men and arms for another grasp at ruling England. All this took place 110 years before our Diarmait's mission. A prized relic from that period was retained in Ferns. It was the battle standard of the king of the Saxons.[3]

After the Battle of Hastings and Harold's death in 1066, there was a repetition of the same enterprise. Harold's sons revolted in 1068 against William the Conqueror and were decisively crushed. They fled to Dublin where the still reigning Mac Máel na mBó again gave them his staunch support and launched a fleet of fifty ships manned by his Leinstermen and Norsemen to take Bristol. The attack was repulsed for 'the Bristol men did not like the Normans but they had still less love for wild Irish kerns and plundering Irish Vikings.' The leader of the English defenders on that occasion was a man named Eadmoth, the portreeve of Bristol. He had once been master of the horse to Harold and a faithful follower but could clearly see the political trend and changed sides. He relentlessly opposed Harold's sons. It was during Eadmoth's earlier service to Harold, at the time when the Leinstermen were hired, that the first contact was made with the Mac Murchadas, but it was by Mac Murchada's men, fighting in Wales for Harold's sons, that Eadmoth himself was slain. This deed took place in June 1069, the occasion of the last Irish military landing in England when the peasants of Somerset rose to obstruct the advancing Leinstermen. The contacts, therefore, between Bristol and Wales, Uí Chennselaig and Leinster had been fostered in peace and in war. Indeed, so thick were relations that through the centuries there was an oratory overlooking the port of Bristol dedicated to St Brendan the Navigator, the Irish patron of all sailors.

Diarmait Mac Máel na mBó and Eadmoth respected one another from the time they had met at the first Leinster assistance to Harold. Although Eadmoth had been killed later by the Leinstermen, the family friendship continued through two generations and the man to whom Diarmait sped, Robert FitzHarding, was the grandson of Eadmoth. Eadmoth's son, Robert FitzHarding had extended the family business and in turn became Bristol's portreeve or chief magistrate. This Robert also had a son named Robert, who was born in 1085 and lived to be eighty-five. It was this man, our Diarmait's friend, who not alone attained prime eminence in Bristol, including the office of portreeve, but also married a girl named Aífe whom one must suspect was a Mac Murchada relation

– for family friendships aside, Norse and Anglo-Norman princes and nobles frequently married the daughters of Irish rulers.

How was FitzHarding at the same time an intimate friend of Henry? When Henry was nine years of age, his father, the count of Anjou, sent him to his uncle in Bristol, the earl of Gloucester. Henry lived in Bristol Castle for four years and there formed his friendship with the chief citizen of that city. FitzHarding had inherited the prudence and foresight of his grandparents and supported Henry in the power struggle with the king Stephen long before his coronation. When Henry came to the throne, he rewarded Robert FitzHarding with the fief of Berkeley which he removed from one of King Stephen's supporters. This was the beginning of the modern earldom of Berkeley which owes its title and descent to Robert FitzHarding. Robert FitzHarding also founded the church and monastery of St Augustine in Bristol for the Canons Regular of St Augustine, dedicated to the Most Holy Trinity, known as Christchurch, and it can be seen to this day with the further added distinction that it was raised to the dignity of a cathedral in the reign of Henry VIII.

Robert FitzHarding's life was one of progress and building. Having lived to be the confidant of kings, he and his wife, in the winter of their days, decided to embrace the monastic life. Robert entered the Augustinian monastery he had founded himself, and this is why it was to St Augustine's that Diarmait sped to lodge with Robert FitzHarding.

This was the man who listened to Mac Murchada, the man who informed him and advised him. It was yet another vital conference (or series of conferences, for Diarmait stayed with Robert FitzHarding until late autumn) of which his secretary, Maurice Ó Regan, gives no account. However Mac Murchada knew the world. He knew of the plan to invade Ireland. He knew what Rome and Europe thought of Ireland's permissiveness and he knew of the papal bull of Adrian, blessing an invasion to right these 'unchristian practices'. He now knew more, for amongst many other assessments Robert FitzHarding told him of the mind of Henry.

SIXTEEN

In Pursuit of a Monarch

Henry II gave every indication that he was a debtor who manoeuvred to avoid his creditor. It took Mac Murchada a long time to lay his hands on him.[1] There were months of searching for the elusive king. Diarmait, accompanied by Maurice Ó Regan, left Robert FitzHarding and Bristol in the late autumn of 1166 to address his requirements to Henry.

Henry had his own pressures. He was engaged in a quarrel with the archbishop of Canterbury, Thomas á Becket. He was also in conflict with the king of France on account of overlapping ambition and expansion. He was having trouble with his subjects in Aquitaine. Neither the atmosphere nor the time was right for Mac Murchada's project. Diarmait landed in Normandy but Henry had departed into the interior. Over the length and breadth of Henry's French dominions from the Pyrenees to the English channel, the monarch avoided the mendicant Irish king. The monarch of the Normans had, in fact, spent Christmas in Poitiers and then rushed off again to the south into Gascony and Guiénne. Where Diarmait spent his first exiled Christmas is not known. The search continued into the new year.

Diarmait and Maurice Ó Regan ultimately overtook Henry and his court in Aquitaine. Mac Murchada contained his frustration while Henry gave no indication that he was aware of any weariness suffered by his visitor. Henry was thirty-four years of age, at the height of his powers and, with thirteen years' experience of the throne behind him, he was rapturously called 'Alexander of the west' by his most affectionate apologist. Impatience boiled unendingly in his blood so that he could 'scarcely spare an hour to hear Mass'.[2] 'Would to God,' a churchman wrote, 'he had been as zealous at his devotions as he was his sports.' He had a red complexion and a large round head. His eyes were grey, blood-shot and flashed in anger. He had a fiery countenance, his voice was tremulous, and his neck a little bent forward; but his chest was broad and his arms were muscular. His body was fleshy and he had an enormous paunch, rather by the fault of nature than from gross feeding. He was well educated but 'fond of hawking and hunting to excess'. Oddly enough, despite his four years in Bristol, he spoke only French.

The Irish king should have been by the hardship of nature past his best. He showed no sign of it. Mac Murchada was still a man of sharp intelligence at fifty-seven years of age. He had an imposing figure which carried authority no matter what his garments, and his apparel before Henry was not as gaudy as it had been two years before. Tall of stature and of stout build, he was a man of warlike spirit, and a brave man, with a voice which had become hoarse from shouting in the din of battle.[3]

Henry received the Irish king cordially and Diarmait saluted him courteously.[4] When the preliminaries were over, Diarmait made his address to Henry and his staff of barons. The churchman Giraldus Cambrensis bestowed an effusive interpretation on Mac Murchada's opening of negotiations.

> *God who dwells on high guard and save you King Henry! May he in the same manner give you heart, courage and the inclination to avenge the shame and the misfortune which my own people have brought upon me! Noble King Henry, hear of where I was born, of what country. Of Ireland I was born a lord, in Ireland I was acknowledged a king. But wrongfully my own people have cast me out of my kingdom. To you, good Sire, I come to make complaint in the presence of the barons of your empire. From henceforth onwards, all of the days of my life I will become your liegeman on condition that you be my ally, so that I will not lose everything. I will acknowledge you as sire and lord in the presence of your barons and earls.[5]*

Mac Murchada had been well informed at Bristol. Before he opened his mouth, he believed that as soon as the king of the Normans had tied up his own loose ends, the full weight of the

Norman soldiers was going to be hurled on Ireland and that the beachhead was in his kingdom of Leinster, and, to be more specific, in his own territory of Uí Chennselaig. Before he entered this conference Diarmait knew that the plans for this invasion were in Winchester and that papal benediction on the enterprise to rectify the 'enormous disorders' had already been bestowed. He knew further the weakness, and also the strength, of the Irish situation. The weakness was that each sub-king or major king was responsible for his own sphere of influence only. Neighbouring Irish kingdoms could be as totally opposed to one another as if they were of different enemy races.

Mac Murchada knew too that this very weakness was Ireland's strength for after, say, the military collapse of Uí Chennselaig, an invader would have to tackle Osraige, then Munster, then Connaught, then the rest of the mid-northern states, Meath and Bréifne, and, with all going well for the invader by the time the last kingdom had parleyed, the first to fall would have licked its wounds and be fit to enter the field again from behind. Ireland had no Byzantium or Rome, the fall of which would herald the collapse of the entire country. Ireland was several states, a never-ending quicksand for hostile foreigners, as indeed it turned out to be.

Mac Murchada knew that if his offer of alliance was accepted it would get rid of the necessity of an invasion; but the granting of experienced mercenaries to him, under his command, from Henry, would at once be the means of his new power, a power that he himself was quite capable of controlling or dispensing with. However Henry II did not have a free hand and he had no army to dispatch to Diarmait's aid. He entertained Diarmait's proposal and requirements and offered to help him considerably as soon as was practically possible. He loaded Mac Murchada with gifts but most important of all, he handed Mac Murchada a clarion call to his subjects everywhere to join the battalions of Uí Chennselaig.[6]

Henry, king of England, duke of Normandy and Aquitaine, count of Anjou, to all his liegemen, English, Norman, Welsh and Scots, and to all nations subject to his sway, greeting. Whensoever these letters shall come onto you, know that we have received Diarmait, prince of Leinster, into our grace and favour. Wherefore, whosoever within the bounds of our territories shall be willing to give him aid as our vassal and liegeman, in recovering his dominion, let him be assured of our favour and licence in that behalf.

It was with a hearty spirit that Diarmait took his leave. On Henry's direct command this time, he was to be entertained and housed by Robert FitzHarding in Bristol. Poverty was over, for now Mac Murchada was a guest of the state and Henry II. All that and the counsel of Robert FitzHarding too.

SEVENTEEN

In the Market for Swords

Diarmait Mac Murchada returned to Robert FitzHarding in Bristol in the late spring of 1167.[1] Here for the first time in six months he and Ó Regan heard accounts of the year's events in Ireland. From the captains and seamen of Leinster – Dublin, Wexford and Waterford – they assembled and interpreted the happenings at home.

Ruaidrí Ua Conchobair had reinforced himself as king of Ireland without opposition. He had divided Munster in two, as his father had done, between the Mac Carthaigs and the Ua Briains. He continued to buy loyalty at high cost.[2] Horses, cattle, glorious robes, left his hands in unprecedented measure for loyal right arms. Twenty-five horses and more cattle to Osraige. A gigantic stipend of cattle for Norse Dublin to be levied off the men of Ireland. Seventy horses to Diarmait Mac Carthaig, king of Desmond. Even Mac Lochlainn's people had been bought. Mac Murchada could but marvel at the extent of Ruaidrí Ua Conchobair's determination, while any dream of Mac Murchada's restoration had not the remotest hope of realisation unless it was fortified with certainty of success. The task his ambition demanded now looked enormous before Mac Murchada's eyes. It did not daunt him. His mission had remained undetected. For all his enemies knew he might well have been a pilgrim in Rome.

In Bristol Mac Murchada anticipated no problem in enrolling recruits. In this major port teeming with men, he had the proclamation of Henry read in the public squares, but the call for help with little reward save Henry's blessing fell upon disinterested ears. This was a shock to the optimistic Mac Murchada. He decided that it would be necessary to proclaim that there would be wages for the swords; money and land. It made no difference. No one was interested. He then approached suitable candidates recommended to him by FitzHarding. But it was all to no avail.[3]

With growing fear Mac Murchada found that no one in Bristol was enamoured with his crusade even when backed with the influence of FitzHarding, the word of their sovereign, or reward. If there were no freebooters to be found in Bristol, FitzHarding at least knew where there were men of desperation and little prospect to whom joining an expeditionary force for loot and land might have an appeal. Across the broad Severn river Norman adventurers clashed with the kings and rulers of Celtic Wales. It was still frontier land which the Normans had penetrated despite persistent armed antagonism. Security was unknown. A battered knight from this bloodily disputed country was identified and contacted. This man had little to lose.[4] The earl of Strigul (modern Chepstow) known to history as 'Strongbow', was a soldier 'whose past was brighter than his prospects, whose blood was better than his brains and whose claims of succession were larger than the lands in his possession'.[5] In the choice of a mercenary chief one could not have picked a man with better qualifications for war and conquest in a foreign land, and it mattered little what land. Strongbow was a man of bankrupt fortunes, for he had committed the indiscretion of backing the wrong horse in the struggle to power of Henry II.[6] And if FitzHarding had reaped the reward of his fidelity, the reverse was true of Strongbow.

On Henry's succession to the throne, Strongbow's earldom of Pembroke was forfeited. As a past antagonist of the king, he had no hope whatever in his own lifetime of advancing his own family's or his personal fortunes. Dyfed, Ceredigion and Carmarthen, his lands won with the sword from the Welsh by his grandfather, father and uncle had been whittled away until all were gone. Strongbow, a widower, was almost the same age as Mac Murchada and, in fact, was in little better a situation than Mac Murchada had been two years previously. As with Diarmait, reverses had honed his mind to cunning. He was of ruddy complexion with freckles. He had grey eyes, feminine features, a weak voice and a short neck. He was tall in build and was courteous in manner. He was regarded as a man 'of great generosity'.[7]

Strongbow was not interested in Mac Murchada's problems or propositions. What were a few acres, or gold for that matter, to him? And what had he to do to win these baubles? Organise and lead a band of mercenaries into a foreign land where the best the Vikings had to show after 300 years was a handful of fortified ghettos where they survived at the whim of their gaelic overlord? Mac Murchada could now identify the barren prospects as he had nothing left with which to trade. He then presented to the widowed knight properties and potentials which he knew were not his to offer. He offered the hand of his daughter, Aífe, little more than thirteen years of age, to Strongbow with the promise that on his, Diarmait's death, Strongbow would succeed him as king of Leinster.[8]

There was a stable of thoroughbred Mac Murchadas in Ferns possessing the sole right to inherit royal power when elected, a fact of which Diarmait was well aware. It included several members of recognised eligibility including his own sons while his brother, Murchad, was currently in place as king of Uí Chennselaig. In Irish law and practice the mere concept of a bankrupt French Norman knight assuming Irish royal power was beneath serious consideration. As for Aífe, her father knew, as all Ireland knew, that were she to repudiate the widower Strongbow after one week of marriage or less, she could do so without impropriety or public displeasure. Irish law and practice catered for such an outcome.

Mac Murchada knew this, knew the political ramifications in his homeland, yet in his dispair he deliberately buried the realities in camouflage. This vision, however, took Strongbow's breath away. These were at last the stakes worth a brace of campaigns. Here was ruling power granted to him and his issue for ever. Here was the replica of the career of his fellow Norman a century before when the throne of Sicily had been claimed and held by one such as he. Even that man had no more than determination and the sword – but Strongbow had this king's daughter to wife, and this king's word.

Mac Murchada and Strongbow had lengthy negotiations before the details of the arrangement were hacked out to their satisfaction. Strongbow's part was formidable.[9] He was to recruit and equip an army of men who would arrive in Uí Chennselaig not later than the spring of the following year, 1168, and they were to aid Diarmait – not simply give him help but bolster him with active military support in 'recovering his kingdom'. Negotiations were duly completed, not in haste but with consideration. The men parted and Mac Murchada's spirit soared as his thoughts at last turned to the moment of return to Ferns.

But there was more to be done, for Mac Murchada had now become certain that nothing must be left to chance. He decided to undertake further recruiting, in the area indicated by FitzHarding, among the leaders across the Severn in Wales who would be most likely to help him. It was a well briefed Diarmait who took his leave for the last time from the friend to whom he owed so much, Robert FitzHarding, now in the last days of his life in the robes of an Augustinian friar.[10]

It was a well-planned schedule which now brought him to St David's in west Wales.[11] It was a port which was less than a day's sailing from his native shore. Indeed, it was something more than that. It was the base of one of the most remarkably bred and related broods in history. Nesta was the name of a princess, the daughter of Rhys ap Tewdwr, 'Rhys the Great', the last independent Celtic king of Wales.[12] She was a woman who roused sexual appetite in men early in the 1100s. Men killed for her, became outlaws for her, went to war for her, a king bedded her as did an unknown stranger while she bred herself the general staff of an expeditionary force.

She first married Gerald of Windsor, by whom she had three sons, William, Maurice and David FitzGerald, and one daughter, Angharat. She was carried off from Gerald by the Welsh chieftain, Owain ap Cadwgan, prince of Powys, children and all. Later she sent the children back. She told her lover: 'If you will have me faithful to you and remain with you, send my children to their father.' Their father repaid the debt when he killed Owain in battle.

There were three more sons and a daughter: William Hay, Hoel and Walter, and Gledoweis.

She became the mistress of the king, Henry I, and bore him a son, the first of all the FitzHenrys. Her son, in turn, fathered Meiler and Robert FitzHenry, all later of Mac Murchada's force. With Stephen, the constable of Cardigan, she had a child, Robert FitzStephen, of whom we will hear more. A granddaughter, also named Nesta, married Harvey de Monte Marisco, Strongbow's uncle. A grandson, William FitzGerald, married Strongbow's daughter Aline. Nesta senior was also grandmother of the first of the Redmond family, Raymond le Gros who joined the expedition to Ireland.

All this brood of ambition, half-Norman and half-Welsh, occupied the area to which Mac Murchada now hastened. He first went to the court of the man recognised by the Welsh as the sovereign of Wales, Rhys ap Gruffydd, nephew of Nesta. In the uneasy truces of the day, this man had recognised Henry II as overlord – but only as long as it suited him. Diarmait's family and that of Rhys had long connections, like the Hardings, because of campaigns over three generations. There was another reason for his visit. A prisoner of note was spending a third year in the dungeons of Rhys Castle.[13] He was Nesta's son, Robert FitzStephen, first cousin of his captor and a legend. He was a man of honour and loyalty to his own. Rhys had offered him liberty if he would but take his sword against his king, Henry, but he refused. Robert FitzStephen was a handsome man, in stature somewhat above middle height. He was bountiful, generous and pleasant, but too fond of wine and woman, according to his ordained and celibate nephew, Gerald. Otherwise, he was 'an excellent man, the true pattern of singular courage and unparalleled enterprise'.

Mac Murchada was received with kindness by the Celtic king of Wales.[14] If the court was not more splendid than Henry's, the material assistance sought and won was magnificent, for the man Mac Murchada now wanted was Robert FitzStephen. FitzStephen was drawn up from his dungeon, the dark and only world he had know since 1165. Ushered before his cousin, he discerned the eyes of Diarmait Mac Murchada. There were two other men present also on this occasion. One was the bishop of St David's, Nesta's son, David FitzGerald; the other was Nesta's other son, the bishop's brother, Maurice FitzGerald. The only one present who was not a close relative to all parties was the intrigued Mac Murchada.

FitzStephen must have been the picture of misery as he was led in, for he had at once the sympathy of his kin, the FitzGeralds. To any man, close confinement is particularly heavy, but to the progeny of Nesta a tomb and an end to the grim solitude were preferable. Mac Murchada knew what Robert FitzStephen's options were. They were the dungeon walls or Ireland as he interceded for his release.[15] The position was laid before the prisoner. Rhys, king of Wales, would give his cousin his freedom on one condition: namely that he place his military talents at Mac Murchada's disposal across the Irish Sea. Robert FitzStephen's half-brothers urged the acceptance of the proposition. For the prisoner it was the first slit of sun to catch his eyes for three summers. He preferred 'committing himself to the chances of fortune and fate at the hazard of his life in a strange country'. He agreed to the terms in consideration of his release, together with as much of a following as he should get. If triumph surged through Diarmait at this prize, he did not show it for in the course of the deliberations it became apparent that there was something better than one hero and that was two heroes. Mac Murchada presented enticements to FitzStephen's cousin, the sympathetic Maurice FitzGerald.

He now uttered a fine-sounding bribe to both Maurice Fitz-Gerald and Robert FitzStephen. Diarmait would grant 'to Robert and Maurice the town of Wexford, with two adjoining baronies of land, to be held in fee; in consideration whereof the said Robert and Maurice engaged to succour him in recovering his territories as soon as spring should come and the winds be favourable'.[16]

Wexford and its southern precincts were Norse, so Diarmait gave away their town; a matter of no consequence to him whatever. As for the adjoining baronies of land, they were regarded as evil-spirit infested bogs and the heartily cursed point of Carnsore. It was a shunned low-lying place of marshes farmed by Norsemen which bore no comparison to the productivity of the soils surrounding Ferns.[17] Mac Murchada gave nothing away but water-logged soil in which only stunted indigenous bushes grew and the furze bush flower farmed as an all purpose crop by the Flemish and Norman settlers. Even today its soil's capacity bears no relation in potential to the rich soils of Mac Murchada's core ruling area on either side of the Blackstairs mountain range.

The half-brothers jumped at the chance. Rhys, infected by the enthusiasm, offered his own son.[18] All gladly accepted, but Mac Murchada, to make assurance doubly sure, aimed his generosity at another race of men, the Flemish exiles of Pembrokeshire.[19] This enclave of Flemings arose because of a disastrous series of storms in the Low Countries the previous century. From their waterlogged homes thousands of Flemings found shelter in Britain but they were always regarded as aliens and constantly shifted until at this period they were concentrated in Pembrokeshire. To these men without a homeland, Diarmait now introduced another successful recruiting drive. What is more, the Flemings were not content to wait for the shift of the political wind. They were prepared to sail for Diarmait's homeland right away.[20]

Nesta's episcopal son, David, now entertained Diarmait. It caused no stir at the time that the bishop had a son, Milo. Milo was also volunteered for the campaign. Diarmait began to hunger for his home and for the restoration of his former honour. With the blood of that prolific mother, the Welsh princess Nesta, in the veins of his general staff Diarmait expected a successful campaign, for every man that Nesta bred was a champion.

EIGHTEEN

To Home

Diarmait Mac Murchada set sail from St David's in Wales around 1 August 1167 for his homeland. With him was his counsellor, Maurice Ó Regan. There were others. There was the son of the king of Wales. There was also a Flemish platoon consisting of knights, archers and sergeants under the command of one Richard FitzGodebert. Since the FitzGodebert castle at Rhos in Pembrokeshire was built on a rock the family was invariably referred to as de la Roche – of the rock – by the French Normans and hence the name which has made a notable contribution to the country of their adoption. So to the Flemish nation went the distinction of providing the latest injection of foreign blood into the Irish race since the establishment 300 years previously of the Norse.[1]

The weather for the voyage home was fair; the wind blowing from the east was favourable. In half a day the excited king leaped into the surf of Uí Chennselaig, under the fort of Glascarrig, almost one year to the day from his flight to Bristol.[2] The effect the small party of Flemish soldiers made has never been commented on except in Maurice Ó Regan's indirect lines: 'They were hardly able to do any good to the king in the land there because they were only a few men who crossed over in a hurry.'

Mac Murchada headed for Ferns. It would have been a lovely time of the year in Ireland, the harvest was near and the golden corn ear weighed heavily against its neighbour in the breeze. Cattle that were wispish in the late winter now had bellyfulls of grass to eat. As Diarmait passed through the woods he knew so well he would, had he been any other Irish monarch, have expected the probability of a coup in his absence. Such a fear is absent from any of the contemporary records. The family loyalty, unique in that century, stood firm. When the embraces were over, Murchad, Diarmait's brother, the man appointed to Diarmait's reduced kingdom of Uí Chennselaig, now gave way as if by arrangement to his elected chief. Diarmait Mac Murchada was home. There were so many things to be done. First the news that he had procured for Aífe a knight in mail for a husband. A fine man, a soldier of fortune, brave, generous, no boy perhaps, but if it didn't work out there was the Brehon law of repudiation. How was Énna, his son to whom he had delegated authority? The son taken a hostage to the enemy Mac Gilla Pátraic of Osraige? Good in health and spirit. Then he had to show his Flemish soldiers as samples of what was to come. The examination of the armour, the weapons, gave spirit to Mac Murchada's men. Richard FitzGodebert or 'de la Roche' was introduced. His new aide-de-camp was to discuss the latest European strategies and moves with him so that when the trial of strength came Mac Murchada and Mac Murchada's men would dovetail into the battle plans.

But there must be silence and discretion. No one was to boast of Diarmait, of the healthy buoyance, of the helmeted men, of the new-awakened hope. If there was a breath of optimism wafted over the mountains all would be lost before battle had even begun. Mac Murchada himself must be hidden and in what better place could a man disappear than in the cloister? Diarmait Mac Murchada entered the monastery he had founded himself for the Canons Regular of St Augustine in Ferns. Here he spent the next winter. The monks entertained him to the best of their ability, but he laid aside his royal dignity and vanished into the privacy of the cell.[3]

The contemplative life Mac Murchada embraced was not entirely devoted to the beatific vision. The vision which the former king of Leinster and the Norse now conjured up was the vision of himself as king of Ireland, avoiding the mistakes of his Celtic brother, Rhys, and keeping his mercenaries in check as vassals. It was a vision which did not conclude with him reaching that kingship. It was a vision which continued with that eminence down through his posterity. If the fates were kind it could be accomplished, for allied to his own men would be these iron-clad auxiliaries with battle strategies developed over years of strife against all races and religions. Mac Murchada had a winter to formulate his plans, and he did not underestimate the obstacles to his restoration.

When he had listened to his last vespers it was spring, As he took the three hundred or so strides to his rebuilt castle he must have pondered on what 1168 would bring. Already his secret was out, for the news of strange soldiers with coloured shields who spoke a language that was not Welsh, Irish, French or Norse had percolated through to the high king's fortress and the houses of his enemies. They knew now that Mac Murchada was with these men and had returned from overseas where they had hoped he was on nothing more menacing than a pilgrimage.

As soon as Mac Murchada's presence on the soil of Uí Chennselaig was confirmed, old apprehension thrived and in a short time an army was assembled whose leaders' names were now familiar and united in their hatred of him: Tigernán Ua Ruairc, the Norse of Dublin, Diarmait Ua Máel Sechlainn of Meath and the high king Ruaidrí Ua Conchobair.[4] The assembled army sped on to Uí Chennselaig and Ferns on the exact route where Diarmait's men had been savaged two years before. On this occasion, however, the weakling who came towards their army at Cill Osnadh was not the defiant Mac Murchada. It was a man past his best with no belly for fight. This Diarmait treated for peace, without contest, indicating that his strength was spent.[5]

Unfortunately a tragedy occurred. While the discussions between Diarmait and his scarcely believing foes took place, Ua Ruairc's men, frustrated in their quest for plunder, attacked the Uí Chennselaig lines. Open battle resulted but the numerically inferior Uí Chennselaig men were overwhelmed. Among the 200 casualties was the son of Rhys, the king of Wales, who was killed. He was described by the Four Masters as 'the son of the king of Britain, who was the battle prop of the island of Britain'.

When the conflict was over the most difficult moment in Mac Murchada's resurgence was reached. However Mac Murchada gave no other impression save that of contrition and this time satisfaction. The high king knew that men under his command – Ua Ruairc's men – had precipitated the outrage. So Mac Murchada was not expelled nor killed nor maimed. At long last, after fourteen years, Mac Murchada dutifully paid one hundred ounces of gold as the honour price, according to the Brehon law, for the 'abduction' of Tigernán Ua Ruairc's wife, Derbforgaill. Secondly, the high king was to be acknowledged as Diarmait's overlord, and hostages were to be given to the high king to ensure the permanence of this arrangement. That was all. The former king of Leinster and the Norse was left in free possession of his core kingdom of Uí Chennselaig. And that, the enemies of Mac Murchada assumed, was that. They withdrew, and Mac Murchada withdrew, now wondering where Robert FitzStephen and Maurice FitzGerald were or what was delaying them.

Despite his cunning and his defiance from the depths, Mac Murchada's Achilles' heel was the regard he had for his offspring. As the end of 1168 drew near and Uí Chennselaig strapped its broken limbs, the ruler of Osraige deposited near Ferns the living body of a man with the blood just beginning to scab over his eyes, which had been pierced by a knife.[6] The man who stumbled towards Diarmait Mac Murchada was Énna his son, whose achievements had already caused him to be noted and recorded as being of ruling potential.

This outrage against a man who to all appearances was broken fired Mac Murchada. No longer content to wait and watch and make ready for another enemy onslaught as soon as the winter's rains had ceased, he summoned his secretary and ambassador, Maurice Ó Regan.[7] Ó Regan was now told to go to Wales, to whip in FitzStephen and FitzMaurice. There were agreements to be implemented. He was ordered to start another recruiting campaign with liberal rewards for volunteers. This he did like a man possessed and he presented Diarmait's letters to earls, barons, knights, squires, sergeants, common soldiers, horse and foot. He preached the word in all directions:

Whoever will wish for land or money, horses, trappings, or chargers, gold or silver; I will give them very ample pay. Whoever will wish for soil or for sod, I will enfeoff them.[8]

In the meantime conditions favourable to Mac Murchada developed. There was the dispatch of Donnchad Ua Cerbaill, the venerable ruler of Airgailla.[9] He was killed while drunk by the axe of his own servant, Ua Duibhne, who, remarkably, who was of the *Cenél nEóghain*, that is one of Mac Lochlainn's own dynasty.

The more significant event, however, took place in Thomond. There the Ua Briain king, Muirchertach, was treacherously eliminated by his own grandnephew upon whose head, in turn, retribution was promptly visited. The man who succeeded as king of Thomond was Diarmait Mac Murchada's son-in-law, Domnall Mór Ua Briain, a man who was to prove himself in many ways as gifted as his great predecessor, Brian Bóruma.[10] And Mac Murchada's daughter was actively at his side. Finally, the year 1168 was a year of increase in crops and therefore the addition of wealth, health and economic security.

Ó Regan's recruiting offensive in Wales faced frustration after months of striving and cajoling because a deterrent had materialised: Henry II had declared his opposition to an independent mercenary enterprise to Ireland. To Robert FitzStephen and Maurice FitzGerald, however, the prospects offered were too good to be dropped. They foraged for the funds and provisions they needed to supply their expedition independently. The two half brothers completed their negotiations in the English city of Gloucester on the upper Severn. There the Jewish merchant, Josce, had sufficient confidence in them to underwrite their military adventure.[11] The expeditionary force was organised, assembled, equipped. Ships were requisitioned and made ready, the chain of command put in order. The overall commander, the man who could see into the future as clearly as Mac Murchada, was Strongbow. He would not travel on the first expedition. The immediate commander of the first expedition was the son of Nesta, Robert FitzStephen, who had escaped rotting to death in his Celtic cousin's prison. FitzStephen assembled a small army of thirty knights of his own kinsmen and retainers, sixty cavalry men in half armour and about 300 archers and foot soldiers, defined as the 'flower of the youth of Wales'. This force was to be taken over in three ships.

A Flemish contingent of volunteers under the command of Maurice de Prendergast was also assembled with two ships to transport them. This group was assembled at Milford Haven and in addition to ten men-at-arms had a considerable body of archers. Both contingents knew exactly the spot on the coast to which they were to go and also how to get there. Getting there was not as simple as the traditional shortest distance between two points. The place chosen by Mac Murchada for the mercenary force to land was Bannow, a strategic inlet on the Atlantic coast of his kingdom, but right around the merciless Carnsore Point on the south-east corner of Ireland.[12] They had to sail out into the Atlantic from Wales to avoid this peril and come back up under the coast of Diarmait's homeland. Bannow was midway between Viking Wexford and Viking Waterford. Harvey de Monte Marisco, travelled with FitzStephen and was noted at once by Nesta's son as 'having neither armour nor money, but was a spy rather than a soldier and as such acted for Strongbow whose uncle he was'.[13] Strongbow was not giving anything away either.

NINETEEN

The Help Arrives

In the first week of May 1169 an Uí Chennselaig soldier rode up the road to Ferns from the south, galloping his horse to foam. He slackened rein at Ferns Castle. Mac Murchada's messenger had remarkable intelligence to report. Over 500 men clad in armour, with helmets which covered the skull and nose, were safely landed on Bannow's foreshore. Many had pennants with shields as well as their emblems, long arrows and bows. They had lances longer than a horse's body with a great many tackled horses, now grazing above Bannow's beach. The soldiers spoke in three different languages, French, Welsh and Flemish. All of them were under the command of a man called Robert FitzStephen.[1]

The time had come for Mac Murchada to cast off the cloak of humility and penitence. Orders were swept around. Soon the eldest son, Domnall Cáemánach Mac Murchada, with an army of 500 Uí Chennselaig men were on their way south to join the auxiliaries of their king. Mac Murchada was not far behind. The Atlantic coast chieftains, Ua Lorcáin and Ua Duiginn, were sub-chiefs of Mac Murchada's and their men rallied now to join him.[2] When Mac Murchada strode forward at the seashore of Bannow he greeted the expedition's leaders with an embrace. Courteously saluting them, he surveyed the first strong contingent of mercenaries, the men who were to help him once more to greatness.[3] They remained there by the waters of Bannow Bay and spoke long into the night by the camp fires. There was a lot of material on the agenda. Firstly, Mac Murchada renewed their former agreements and confirmed them under oath.[4] Secondly, they joined their forces into a united battle plan, and, lastly, they had to decide where, under the conditions of the moment, they were to attack.

The Norse knew from their frequent shipping contacts that an expedition was being mounted. Where it was to strike they did not know, but of the three Norse cities to choose from – Waterford, Dublin or Wexford – the choice was almost inevitable. The fortified port of Wexford was the threat from the immediate rear to be reduced. In addition there was nothing like prompt reward to encourage a man like FitzStephen. So to Wexford the army of four races marched, coloured and arrayed. Tradition says that a skirmish at Dun Cormick was the only ripple on the way but an army such as this in battle array does not invite an impromptu assault.[5] With Mac Murchada in command an attack from a local Irish source could only have been due to a misunderstanding. There was, however, a Norse enclave at Clonmines in Bannow Bay and the arrival of the ships, the men, and the armed hundreds from Ferns would certainly have caused a party to reconnoitre.[6]

Wexford knew in advance of the approach of the army of Mac Murchada. The finger points to the Norsemen of Clonmines as responsible for this intelligence. Wexford mustered twice the number of men that Mac Murchada had in his command and its leaders decided that it would be far more profitable to overwhelm Mac Murchada's 1100 in the open field than to endure a siege again. Wexford had never in its history been taken by storm and even if some foe did breach their walls they had the open sea and a safe harbour to escape. From the heights at the back of Wexford the sight the Viking eyes fell on was discomforting. Alongside Mac Murchada, with his men bearing the familiar Irish weapons of the day, they viewed a martial avalanche with four distinct types of soldiers. There were in addition to the Irish foot soldiers, archers, horsemen with lances and shields and swordsmen. Perhaps a siege might not be so boring after all. They retreated to the security of their walls but first of all they razed to the ground the dwellings of the Irish inhabitants outside them.[7]

As Mac Murchada contemplated the blazing homes before Wexford, he realised that he was embarked upon an enterprise in which he had no experience, namely the taking of a fortified town by storm. However this didn't present a problem as there were now specialists in his camp. This was one facet of military tactics in which any veteran of a Norman campaign excelled. FitzStephen was the man for the task.[8] He lined the trenches in front of the walls with those of his troops who wore armour. The archers were posted on the rock terrace of Carrigeen facing the Norse wall 100 yards away across the graveyard of St Peter's where today's Garda barracks find their macabre foundations. Sheets of arrows rained on the Norsemen while the assault commenced with sustained vigour. The men, hungry for victory, raised the scaling ladders against the walls. Wexford had never been taken and the Vikings returned with interest everything they got on that first assault. The Norsemen fought for their 300-year-old independent port town with fanatical zeal. They cast down from the battlements a hail of beams and rocks and repulsed with vigour the best that FitzStephen could offer. FitzStephen decided to try again, but the next day would be time enough.[9]

Eighteen of Mac Murchada's army were killed while the Wexford defenders lost only three. Nesta's grandson, Robert de Barry, almost had his skull knocked in and was rescued with difficulty from the trench in under the wall. After this reverse it was decided that there would be as few ships as possible left for the Vikings to use so a rush was made for the ships on the strands which stood on either side of the fortified town. The fleet was put to fire (the coat of arms of Wexford today consists of three blazing ships). One band of Mac Murchada's landlubbers received a fright when they boarded a British merchantman loaded with corn and wine. It was moored in the harbour and as the intrepid firebrands went to work the crew cut the hawsers from the anchors and off they went under their own power. Since the wind was blowing from the west the ship gathered speed and soon the warriors found Wexford a lot more close to the horizon than they wished. It was only with the greatest difficulty after they leaped into their boats that they eventually returned to their comrades.

Next morning before the walls of Wexford there was a full parade of all Diarmait's army for Mass. It was thought that it would have a good psychological effect on the besieged. Of this

Mac Murchada was certain for already inside the walls of Norse Wexford was Diarmait's own bishop of Ferns, Joseph Ua hÁeda. We do not know how long he was there or his stated business, or why the ghetto Vikings entertained him, but there he was. He was in his own right, as he proved on another day, no simpleton. FitzStephen set about the task of taking Wexford with all the skill and experience that Norman arms could provide. He deployed his men to much better effect and studied the formation of the defences. He appealed to their skill, and this time to their courage, for the task was not going to be easy. Indeed, for FitzStephen as well as for Mac Murchada, fortune had been capricious and it was with a large question mark looming that Diarmait watched the proceedings. His army drew near to the walls. Suddenly abandoning hope, seeing the meticulous planning, and the menace in their enemies the Norse decided to sue for peace. Of the two chroniclers of the events of the siege, Diarmait's Maurice Ó Regan reports the Norsemen as traitors. The Welsh account offers us more detail: the Norsemen 'reflecting that they were disloyally resisting their prince sent envoys to Diarmait commissioned to treat of the terms of peace'. Diarmait's bishop now enters the stage. By the mediation of the bishop, Ua hÁeda, terms were arranged. Had the Vikings been aware of Diarmait's munificence in promising their town to FitzStephen they would have taken to the walls again. For the terms as agreed sold their independence forever.

The Norse of Wexford submitted to Diarmait as their king. They gave him four hostages as insurance for that loyalty and their armed forces were now at Mac Murchada's command. The town was saved. There was no pillage, looting or rape worth recording. Diarmait and his almost untried army entered the town, one of the three most important citadels of commerce in Ireland. It was a great moment for Mac Murchada because it was the kerbstone of victory to come. It was also a defence if the worst came to the worst and his back was to the wall once more. Outside of his own ranks, there were no specialists in the art of taking a walled town by storm.

To the ex-prisoner, the son of Nesta, Robert FitzStephen, and *(in absentia)* his half-brother, Maurice FitzGerald, went the town of Wexford. Diarmait also bestowed those two gardens of rush and sally tree, the dependent baronies of the town to the south on them. To Strongbow's eyes and ears in Ireland Harvey de Monte Marisco, went two other regions adjoining the sea between Wexford and Norse Waterford. It included the ruling area of the family that betrayed him without pity, Ua Brain, after whom the modern barony of Shelbourne is named.[10]

With all these generosities accomplished and a trouble-free hinterland as far as the mountains, Mac Murchada thought it well to give his army time to recuperate. The entire army, except the Vikings, withdrew to Ferns where they spent the next three weeks basking in the sun and absorbing the examination of Mac Murchada's people.

TWENTY

Hell to Osraige

One of the first things to excite the curiosity of any visitor to Diarmait's castle would have been the sight of his blinded son. Énna was young in blindness and would not have learned the craft of the long blind. Over the three weeks of the army's rest Énna's plight weighed heavily on his father. At the end of the rest, therefore, Mac Murchada did not strike north as his mind was on taking revenge on Osraige and its ruler, Mac Gilla Pátraic.[1] There was another reason too. Osraige's strength would have to be neutralised before Diarmait could take his army for a campaign against all comers. He had few spare men for garrison work, and Osraige was alongside him, they were bitter foes and regarded each other with mutual hatred.[2] When he proposed to subdue Osraige the motion was agreed by FitzStephen and the Flemish leader, de Prendergast. The geographical details were left to Mac Murchada. As for his army, he now had the reluctant support of the Norsemen of Wexford, a factor which put his nominal strength in the field at approximately 3,000.

The assault on Osraige was carried out with such slaughter and efficiency that no one was unaffected by the carnage. Not even the seasoned Fleming, de Prendergast. Diarmait's advance into an Osraige was well flagged and his new spearhead was no surprise.[3] He went in through the pass of Gowran and found a fortified earthwork. A barricade consisting of a 'triple fosse and vallum and on top of each vallum a stockade of branches' was erected across the pass. Behind this stockade the ruler of Osraige lay in waiting with a reported 5,000 men, 2,000 more than Diarmait could muster. This, then, was to test the worth of his hired arms.

The battle for the barricade, which started the following morning, lasted into the evening. Ultimately, it was FitzStephen's men who broke through – but not without losses. Once through the barricade the day seemed to be with Mac Murchada but the king of Osraige rallied his men behind the route which Diarmait's army was using to withdraw back home. Domnall Cáemánach Mac Murchada and his Uí Chennselaig men had been through this before and, fearing another trap, withdrew to cover. This exercise created a position of peril. Alone, except for a small contingent of 45 men, a Norman knight found himself vulnerable to their enemies. De Prendergast, who was in command of Diarmait's auxiliaries in the sector, set to work to rescue them. He ran his men towards the nearby heights where his horsemen could group and charge in formation. He then set up a line of archers in a grove to shoot death in hails.

The men of Osraige had different ideas. They took up the pursuit of the Flemish but when the heights were reached de Prendergast's men turned abruptly around and attacked their pursuers with fury. The Osraige men involved were felled. Speared with lances, scattered and running, they now had to face Mac Murchada's own regrouped soldiers. These created havoc with their broad axes. No one who could offer resistance was spared. The price exacted for Énna's eyes was heavy.

Mac Murchada rested at the banks of the river Barrow. From the Welsh accounts of the day's events now comes a description of an aftermath so bizarre as to invite disbelief.[4] It is not in any other contemporary account, and Irish annalists do not neglect atrocities. It goes as follows:

> Over two hundred Osraige men's heads were produced and displayed to Diarmait. He turned them over and examined them, one by one. On one occasion he clapped his hands and leaped for joy and giving God thanks burst into a triumphant song. But one other head which he recognised, one whom he hated above the rest, he took up by the ears and hair and in a most blood-thirsty and brutal manner tore away with his teeth the lips and the nose.

FitzStephen now proposed to Diarmait that the army encamp by the Barrow for the night and finish the process of demolition of

Osraige the next day, but Mac Murchada marched his men for rest to the monastic settlement of St Laserian at Old Leighlin, a prominent site on a hill two miles west of the river. The following day Mac Murchada's forces returned to Ferns for a short breathing space.

The wonder of the battle for Osraige and, for that matter, Wexford, was that numerically superior forces had been overwhelmed by Mac Murchada's army using better tactics. The message now percolated throughout the land and these victories brought chieftains who had abandoned Diarmait back to allegiance. Mac Murchada was becoming feared. The pre-Mac Murchada ruling families of Leinster would not yet accept the return to power of Mac Murchada. While that might have been tolerated moderately a decade ago, now Mac Murchada could not indulge anyone.[5] So he turned upon the north Leinster territories of Ua Fáeláin and his brother-in-law Ó Tuathail. With their allegiance now grudgingly restored and the ruler of Ua Fáeláin banished, he turned his attention once more on the battered but unrepentant king of Osraige, the 'most powerful as well as the most irreconcilably hostile of his tributaries'.

Assembling every available man and weapon Mac Murchada set out from Ferns in command of the ultimate campaign against Osraige. His son, Domnall Cáemánach Mac Murchada, led the vanguard. Next came the Norsemen of Wexford, and lastly, in the rear, came the Welsh-Normans and the Flemish. They crossed into Osraige near Old Leighlin and marched unopposed to the then turbulent river at Freshford. On the opposite bank on his own chosen and well-fortified battlefield waited Mac Gilla Pátraic, king of Osraige, and his men. Mac Murchada's men encamped for the night on the river's bank.

From this night another one of those bizarre incidents which were a feature of the Welsh account is given to us.[6] It involved two of Nesta's grandsons (one of them a son of her child by Henry I), Robert de Barry and Meyler FitzHenry. These two were part of a contingent of Welsh-Normans who had the temerity to encamp in an old Irish rath. Suddenly in the middle of the night 'there was a great noise as it were of many thousands of men rushing in upon them from all sides with a great rattling of arms and clashing of battleaxes'. The Welsh writer of the 1100s goes on to explain to the reader that 'such spectral appearances frequently occur in Ireland to those who are engaged in hostile excursions'. The alarm was raised with such vehemence that men were soon in confusion, running for cover, racing across marshes, up trees and behind bushes with such open eyed fright as if the army of Osraige had appeared in their very middle. Robert de Barry restored order, it is recorded, 'to the admiration as well as the envy of many'.

Ghosts or no ghosts, Mac Murchada forded the river at dawn and attacked the heavily defended enemy camp. In the spearhead of the attack were the reluctant Norsemen of Wexford. The fight had been beaten out of the Wexford Norse. They knew they were finished after over 300 years in Wexford. They had not the heart for the job, an attitude dismal to record, for in previous campaigns once the Vikings were committed they fought with fury. For three days they were allowed to half-heartedly pick away at the Osraige stockade, but their efforts petered out uselessly. Mac Murchada tossed the storming specialists into the attack. The Norman-Welsh and Flemings succeeded in a short space of time in breaching the stockade and unleashing once more Mac Murchada's battleaxes and torches on Osraige. The Osraige men fled, for there was no defence against the long-distance marksmanship of the archers or the mail-clad cavalry allied to the Uí Chennselaig footsoldiers. Mac Murchada chased Mac Gilla Pátraic to the extremity of his territory but failed to lay his hands on him. It was better for him that he did not.

Diarmait returned with his army to Ferns laden with the spoils of war. He mused on what he could accomplish with these mercenaries. The leader of the Flemish contingent, de Prendergast was, however, undergoing a crisis of confidence. Although he could scarcely credit it, Pembrokeshire, for all its disadvantages, was a garden compared to Ireland. Here it seemed as though every neighbouring state, though Irish, was prepared to fight and die to the last man against another. Was it worth it to him or to his people? He decided it was not.

Mac Murchada, who had become used to crises was faced with a battalion desertion, and one which had covered itself with distinction since its arrival. De Prendergast informed Diarmait at Ferns that he had seen enough, had had enough, and was withdrawing with the Flemish contingent back to Wales.[7] This came as a blow to Mac Murchada. The campaign was at a critical stage and was, in fact, only beginning. However he could not dissuade de Prendergast, and the Flemish knight with his contingent of 200 men evacuated Ferns down the riverside road to the port of Wexford some 25 miles distant. Mac Murchada had to act fast. He had a rider in the port of Wexford before de Prendergast with his orders to the captain of every ship that no one was to transport the de Prendergast battalion to Wales. When the Flemish soldiers arrived in Wexford their fate was sealed. They were outmanoeuvred and cut off by a fifty-mile-wide moat from the land of their adoption.

However a campaigner of de Prendergast's quality is never outmanoeuvred. If he had to stay he would no longer serve Mac Murchada. So bitter was he at the drawbridge Mac Murchada had raised before his face that he decided on something which could not have had more conceivable peril for the man who hired him. He offered his army and his men to Osraige.[8]

TWENTY-ONE

A Son for the High King's Daughter

Whatever his resources were Mac Gilla Pátraic offered de Prendergast 'safe conduct' and solemnly promised him 'ample reward', in the same manner that Diarmait had previously.[1] De Prendergast and his men withdrew from Wexford unhindered by the Norsemen and started out on the danger filled trek to Osraige through Diarmait's homeland. On a narrow defile between two hills lay the pass of Poulmonty into Osraige. To this spot Diarmait now detailed Domnall Cáemánach Mac Murchada to block de Prendergast's passage. De Prendergast, desperate before his new enemies and with no illusions about his fate if caught by Mac Murchada, hacked his way through the pass. After three days Mac Gilla Pátraic joined de Prendergast at the old ecclesiastical stronghold of St Mullins and in solemn speech undertook under oath upon the altar of St Moling 'never to betray Maurice de Prendergast or his men'.

Once more Mac Murchada's sword-won Irish allies began to ask themselves if he could possibly survive. The answer seemed to be in the negative. One man, however, who had become very impressed with Mac Murchada was the released prisoner, Robert FitzStephen. Even he, with his now small band of less than 300 men, was not strong enough to ward off another swamping attack on Diarmait Mac Murchada if anyone planned his destruction. However there was another question rattling through Mac Murchada's head: where was Strongbow? Where were the rest of the men who were, or should have been by now, recruited? All that was required to restore Leinster and Dublin to him, and for that matter the high kingship itself, was another couple of thousand mercenaries. Where were they?

Before that question could be investigated Mac Murchada was pushed again upon the razor's edge. The story of his defeat of much heavier forces was the talking point of Ireland. So, too, was the minute size of the battalion of mercenaries he had hired. The high king, Ruaidrí Ua Conchobair, could no longer disregard the accounts and so at last he organised an army to investigate and overwhelm Mac Murchada who now, whether it was known widely or not, had very little firm ground to stand on. Correctly, then, the high king and the force he assembled deemed the Flemings, as they incorrectly described FitzStephen's puny squadron, 'as not worth notice'.[2]

The army of the high king included the familiar foes of Mac Murchada: Tigernán Ua Ruairc, Diarmait Ua Máel Sechlainn of Meath and the Norsemen of Dublin. The king of Osraige and de Prendergast started to raid Uí Chennselaig; although the rank-and-file in Osraige were very discontented that they had to hire soldiers and actually give them pay.[3] Mac Murchada was forewarned of the coming attack. Instead of seeking to stop or fight this new army in a mountain pass, he and FitzStephen chose a new battlefield.[4] It was the forest between Ferns and the mountains known as the *Dubhtír* or 'Black Country' because of the darkness induced by its closed foliage. The name persists today though it is now open fields. In the 1100s, however, it was a booby trap of marshes, strong trees and thickets, a happy battlefield for those who knew its trails and layout intimately. The battlefield was prepared. Trees were felled, the underwood was plashed, the surface of the level ground was torn up by digging deep pits and trenches, and numerous secret and narrow passages were cut through the thick foliage in many places to provide rapid entry and exit as the progress of the battle demanded. The net result of this piece of engineering was that the defensive properties of this forest were considerably enhanced and, more important still, the defences succeeded in shutting out the enemy while access and exit were open to Mac Murchada and his men. Now the numerically weak king stood a chance of success. It was with buoyant resolve that Mac Murchada and his men awaited the arrival of the high king's army.

Ruaidrí Ua Conchobair, undisputed king of Ireland, commanded the army in person. In some ways he was a very complacent man, different from his father who had never shrunk from the possibility of annihilation. He was not foolishly eager however, when the gauntlet was thrown down. He did not rush his men into the Mac Murchada complex. He spotted that it was Mac Murchada's chosen battlefield; a dark grim hazard for an army on the offensive. The high king decided to negotiate.

Ruaidrí chose to approach the Welsh-Norman knight Fitz-Stephen first. This was the first confrontation between the strongest ruler of Ireland and the new foreigners. Enormous pressure was then applied to FitzStephen to abandon Mac Murchada. Valuable rewards were proffered, and every conceivable argument was put forward to induce FitzStephen to return to Wales with his men in peace and friendship. FitzStephen adamantly refused and from that uncompromising position he could not be induced to budge.

The high king then elected to negotiate with Diarmait Mac Murchada. In all his dealing with the king of Leinster, especially if one considers the background to the cause and situation at the time of such dealings, Ruaidrí Ua Conchobair showed peculiar magnanimity. It is peculiar because with lesser men and with other rulers Ruaidrí showed little scruple. The question remains: why the velvet glove for Mac Murchada? Never once did he attempt to mutilate or kill him and it is certain that if it were not for Ruaidrí on a previous occasion Ua Ruairc would certainly have mutilated or killed Mac Murchada.

Ruaidrí urged Diarmait to unite with him in exterminating the new foreigners and if he did, guaranteed the full restoration to him of the kingship of Leinster and the Norse, with the high king's friendship. Here was a bloodless passage to former glory offered to Mac Murchada, the only price for which was the sword for Robert FitzStephen and his band. What was Mac Murchada's reaction to this proposal? What should his answer be? Had he any honour? Or was he an opportunist at any price? What was a battle comrade if for a mere 250 heads or so of outsiders he could once again don the robes of Leinster – and eliminate the owners of the port of Wexford? Did he think of the Norman hordes from the Pyrenees to the Irish Sea who would revenge such betrayal, or did he consider the peril to his own life if he refused the offer?

Refuse the offer he emphatically did. He would not betray his comrade. So the situation was wide open again and a major battle was looming. Another element intervened at this stage on Diarmait's behalf and that was his bishop and clergy.[5] If Joseph Ua hÁeda had negotiated a victory over the army of the Wexford Norsemen, there was no reason why a similar essay here would not be just as beneficial. The conclusion of the negotiations which followed can only be summed up as one of the remarkable leniencies in history unless one admits that Ruaidrí Ua Conchobair, king of Ireland, held Diarmait Mac Murchada in high regard. The terms were that Diarmait Mac Murchada should be restored to his former position, that of king of Leinster and the Norse. Secondly, that he should acknowledge Ruaidrí Ua Conchobair as high king and render him the appropriate submission.

Diarmait had to hand over to Ruaidrí as hostages for his submission three men whom he loved, for if he had not loved them they would have had little significance as hostages. They were the son of his foster brother, Ua Cáellaide; next his married grandson, that is the son of Domnall Cáemánach Mac Murchada, and lastly, his youngest son of great promise, Conchobar Mac Murchada. To these young men the idea of travelling with the high king would have been interesting as Connaught was so remote and different from Leinster. However there was a more significant clause in the agreement which would have pleased any man, on first examination, that is. Ruaidrí Ua Conchobair promised on his part that if Diarmait remained faithful to his submission he would give his daughter to Conchobar Mac Murchada in marriage.

Ruaidrí Ua Conchobair was not a fool and at this stage Diarmait was his equal in the skills of parleying. If Conchobar Mac Murchada married the high king's daughter it was more than likely that he, Diarmait, had not the remotest chance of obtaining high kingship. He would be also be a sure ally of the high king

Ua Conchobair's dynasty, much more tightly involved than he had ever been previously with Mac Lochlainn.

Mac Murchada and Ruaidrí Ua Conchobair publicly proclaimed and confirmed the conditions agreed upon. There was in addition, however, a secret agreement between the two kings to the effect that Diarmait would bring no more Norman mercenaries into Leinster and further that he should return those he had hired back to Wales as soon as Leinster had been restored to order by him. All piously agreed by Mac Murchada.

The armies parted. The three hostages bade their families goodbye. Mac Murchada thanked God for the new lease of life and the breathing space. As he watched his real enemies depart in the Ua Conchobair van, he looked for the last time on one who would pester him no more. Diarmait Ua Máel Sechlainn, ruler of Meath, nephew of Derbforgaill, Diarmait's old amour, of the family with which he once enjoyed such friendship, had his throat slit by his nephew, Domnall of Bregia, as soon as he returned home. The name of the assassin's accomplice is significant. It was Donnchad Chennselaig Ua Cáellaide.[6]

TWENTY-TWO

The Restoration in Leinster

Mac Murchada now considered recent events. He tried to decipher their significance from the recognition of his rights by the high king to the promise of the high king's daughter to his son in marriage. The conclusion he reached was that he had become the rival for the high kingship and that Ruaidrí desired his friendship far more than his opposition. Therefore, even to Ruaidrí, the possibility of Mac Murchada triumphing over Ireland with his new allies and strategy was real. Mac Murchada fed on the thought and his imagination was fired anew with the dream, now a feasible proposition provided he had more hired arms and men.

To his satisfaction he heard of the arrival in Wexford of two shiploads of reinforcements under the command of Nesta's son, Maurice FitzGerald, FitzStephen's half-brother. The party consisted of ten knights, thirty mounted cavalrymen and roughly 100 archers.[1] It was enough for the time being to replace the defected Flemish men.

The Flemish contingent were busy earning their Osraige wages.[2] Their activities consisted of forays into the weaker portions of the kingdom of Leinster to which Mac Murchada had been restored. One of the persecuted was Ua Mórdha of Laoighis. He was compelled to submit to Osraige but he delayed the delivery of hostages for three or four days and sent for help to Mac Murchada. Mac Murchada lost no time devising a trap for Osraige and the Flemish. He gave FitzGerald his first outing. With Uí Chennselaig's men plus FitzStephen and FitzGerald, he sped to Laoighis, but de Prendergast, identifying Mac Murchada's army spiked with Norman shields, took to his heels, and was pursued into the maze of Osraige's defences. The Osraige chiefs themselves were now weary of a kept, paid army and they decided to eliminate the Flemish.

This plot was aborted by the Flemish themselves. After lulling Mac Gilla Pátraic into a belief in their unswerving devotion they fled to Waterford as fast as their horses could be spurred where they embarked for home, 'Sorrier,' as the cliché has it, 'and wiser men.'

There were things to be done by Diarmait. There was the restoration to normality of Leinster, and his restoration to the vital kingship of Dublin. Early in the spring of 1170 Diarmait neared his sixtieth birthday. The winter rains had imposed a period of leave and planning on him and his military organisers, the foremost of whom were now, Murchad, his brother; Domnall Cáemánach Mac Murchada, FitzStephen whom he trusted and Maurice FitzGerald. Of Harvey de Monte Marisco very little is recorded at this time but his function was to provide his nephew, Strongbow, with sufficient intelligence. Shipping between Wales, Bristol and Wexford continued as before, so passage of information continued unabated. Harvey de Monte Marisco himself, no less than any other adventurer, would have as little trouble shipping across to Wales for a few days' leave for briefing or reporting as they would today. Wexford is nearer to Wales almost by half than it is to Dublin.

The fresh army of Mac Murchada set out for Dublin with hope that was renewed as the new growth on the trees. With the high king giving him a free hand in Leinster, Diarmait could afford this expedition without the help of Robert FitzStephen. FitzStephen was left at home on another mission that was to prove vital, the reconstruction of a defensible fortress on the heights guarding the Slaney ferry at Carraig two miles outside Norse Wexford.[3] Mac Murchada and his army reached the outskirts of Dublin and stopped at the Scandinavian suburbs outside the walls. This area was known as Dyflinarkskirri.[4]

It might have appeared to his hired officers that Diarmait preferred to be 'feared rather than loved' and that 'his hand was against everyman and everyman's hand against his', but they could not have known of his life's vicissitudes nor the spectacle of the numerous desertions of his tributary kings three years before. Norse Dublin was in the latter category and Mac Murchada, who now strode grimly towards their citadel, was not the magnanimous king who had reigned without care a decade before. He was a changed man with no incentive to restrain his instinct to give no quarter.

The Norsemen had the situation assessed. In case they had not Mac Murchada fired the suburbs. There was no battle, no siege. The Norse of Dublin, under their king, Asculv the son of Ragnall, submitted to Diarmait as their overlord and gave him gifts and security for their future fidelity. They, too, had bought time, but, once more, Diarmait Mac Murchada was king of Leinster and the Norse.[5]

A problem blotted Mac Murchada's plans.[6] His son-in-law, Domnall Ua Briain, king of the vital region of Munster, was in trouble with Ruaidrí Ua Conchobair the high king. Domnall Ua Briain had withdrawn his recognition from Ruaidrí Ua Conchobair as high king and Ruaidrí was about to hurl himself upon his throat having already executed Ua Briain's hostages. Domnall appealed urgently for help to his father-in-law. Mac Murchada needed Munster but he had also to maintain excellent relations with the high king until he was in an impregnable position. No matter what he did he could once more be faced with disaster. It required the judgement of a Solomon.

Mac Murchada sent for his trusted FitzStephen and briefed him on the situation. The result of their deliberations was that FitzStephen was dispatched as an unattached freebooter all the way to Limerick with his contingent. FitzStephen's contingent needed luck. Ruaidrí launched a fleet of ships on the Shannon and harried and burned Munster at will. However, the end result of the contest was that Ruaidrí withdrew and Mac Murchada's son-in-law and his sphere of influence were safe for the time being – and Mac Murchada officially had not lifted a finger.

Mac Murchada had now, with the help of not more than 600 mercenaries from overseas, become master of Leinster from Dublin to the Atlantic and had the alliance of his son-in-law, Domnall, king of Munster's Thomond. Yet he saw the weakness of his position despite being buttressed by a few hundred professional soldiers and no matter how invincible he appeared to his neighbours. No one knew better than he that it would be necessary to augment his Uí Chennselaig men with many hundreds of hired soldiers if the idea of all Ireland power was to be entertained.

The limit of his agreement with Ruaidrí Ua Conchobair was now reached. Mac Murchada was now consolidated as king of Leinster, its Norsemen and Dublin. The high king would require the hired help to be sent home. What a hope! The only one who would be sent away if Mac Murchada could help it was the high king. At sixty years of age he could no longer wait for power to fall into his lap. The time had now come to unfold to FitzStephen and FitzGerald the plan already known to his own nearest, the plan for all Ireland power.

To the Welsh-Norman knights this was new and unexpected fare.[7] They were hired to restore Mac Murchada to Leinster. All Ireland was another matter, a whole country with numerous traps, rulers and armies, bigger than Wales. Mac Murchada set to with every power of persuasion, of cunning, of reward, upon the sons of Nesta. The size of the venture was discussed, the size of the opposing armies, the certainty of a campaign in Ulster and Connaught, the probable numbers that Diarmait could enrol in his army from the Norsemen in Leinster and Munster. Mac Murchada was now close to FitzStephen. The fact that FitzStephen was married was of minor interest to Mac Murchada and of little importance by Brehon law. As a token of his respect and admiration for FitzStephen Mac Murchada offered his daughter Aífe to FitzStephen as his wife.[8] This obviously rendered his offer to Strongbow an empty promise. He, FitzStephen, could not according to his law avail of this magnificent gesture. FitzGerald was in a similar position. In addition there was the matter of Aífe's betrothal to Strongbow, if such it was.

They started to examine the proposal of all Ireland conquest with serious intent and after deliberation came to one firm conclusion.

The project could be achieved provided, and only provided, Mac Murchada received reinforcements from Wales. The time had arrived to make demand upon Strongbow's word and promises.

Had Mac Murchada forgotten the three men who were the hostages for his fidelity to the high king, the son of his foster brother, his grandson and his own son? No, he had not forgotten. He calculated, and correctly, that in a position of weakness the high king would not dare to lay a hand on his son. A man who in a position of superiority actually admitted defeat to an outnumbered foe, as Diarmait had been the previous year, instead of cutting them down to the last man, would never, never risk his life by executing the son of a powerful and revitalised Mac Murchada. There was the price Osraige paid for Énna's eyes for all to see.

TWENTY-THREE

Strongbow

Diarmait Mac Murchada dispatched emissaries to Strongbow. They carried a written message. The gist of it, according to FitzStephen's nephew, was as follows:

> *Diarmait, son of Murchada, king of Leinster; to Richard, Earl Gilbert, son of Earl Gilbert, sends greetings.*
>
> *... Neither winds from the east nor the west have brought us your much desired and long expected presence. Let your present activity make up for this delay and prove by your deeds that you have not forgotten your engagements but only deferred their performance. The whole of Leinster has already been recovered, and if you come in time with a strong force the other four parts of the kingdom will be easily united to the fifth. You will add to the favour of your coming if it be speedy; it will turn out famous if it is not delayed, and the sooner the better welcome. The wound in our regards which has been partly caused by neglect will be healed by your presence; for friendship is secured by good offices and grows by benefits to greater strength.[1]*

This letter agitated Strongbow. As with FitzStephen a new and formidable enterprise was being proposed by Mac Murchada, an enterprise which far outstripped the ambition of recovering Leinster. That was already accomplished, but now the king of Leinster wanted all Ireland. Strongbow knew of every move and every phase won since the small batch under FitzStephen went to Leinster. He could see the prospect of success in Ireland under Mac Murchada, but yet at his age to pioneer a hard campaign in a foreign land was not a prospect to be jumped at. He decided on one last proposition to Henry his king and requested an audience to present his request.[2]

Henry had little regard for Strongbow. When the disgraced

baron petitioned his monarch either to restore him to his former lands, if his majesty was pleased, the lands which were his by hereditary right, or to grant him leave to seek his fortune under the Irish king, Henry's reaction was to resort to levity. The words which were delivered in jest rather than in earnest were to the effect that Strongbow could certainly seek his fortune under the Irish king – 'as far as his feet could bear him'. It was from this that Strongbow had to draw his conclusions.

The conclusion which Strongbow drew was that the king had acknowledged him an aged expendable and wished him out of his domain, sweating in some Irish morass. This prospect amused the king who was half Strongbow's age. The other conclusion to be drawn was that Strongbow had not the faintest hope of ever regaining his confiscated Welsh lands. The rage of this battered knight revitalised the soldier's spirit in him. There were knights before such as he, some of them not fit to lead his horse, who had carved out kingdoms for themselves from Antioch to Rome and without half the foothold that he had. Strongbow started to recruit for a great expedition to join Mac Murchada's army. He hired from the west of England, Normans, Flemish, Welsh. It took him a considerable time but he had the first of his ships ready, equipped and sailing under a trusted hand by the beginning of the spring of 1170.[3]

Strongbow's man, Raymond FitzGerald, another grandson of the Welsh princess Nesta, nicknamed 'Raymond le Gros', was given his first strategic mission by Mac Murchada. He was to land, secure and fortify the bronzeage fortifications called Dun Donnell at the mouth of Bannow Bay on Wexford's Atlantic coast. It was situated in the Ua Brain territory and possessed a facility well known to all Uí Chennselaig seafarers. There was deep water all the way to the beach, which resembled in practice a raised quayside or pier. Raymond set sail and landed without difficulty ten knights and seventy archers. It looked a pitiful, small contribution.

Raymond was in trouble, for although Waterford was the target, unless Strongbow arrived in the vicinity with reinforcements he was isolated, a sitting target for the Osraige men and the Waterford Vikings. He could not even be sure of immediate support from Diarmait's army miles away from what came to be known as Baginbun. He therefore worked with the energy born of alarm to entrench, fortify and expand the defensive properties of that craggy little peninsula. He then took precautions against hunger by stealing cattle and driving them into his stockade. With the rich May growth, keeping them alive was no problem and they had a fresh water supply nearby. In short, he had a well-chosen sanctuary to wait for more favourable winds which would bring Strongbow across with many more troops to join Mac Murchada. Harvey de Monte Marisco on being informed of the sailing and destination went down to Baginbun with three men from Wexford and joined Raymond. They were not given much time to relax.

The Waterford Norsemen, the Osraige men and the Deise ruler, Ua Fáeláin, determined on the extermination of the overseas adventurers, for they were convinced beyond doubt that they were next in line as soon as Mac Murchada's army joined Raymond's battalion. The Waterford and Osraige leaders reputedly assembled between them about 3,000 men for the task[4]. When this multitude bore down on Raymond he instantly, in desperation, ordered an attack, but his men had to turn tail and run for their lives. Pressing home the advantage, however, the triumphant army made the fatal mistake of bunching together like a congregation in a church exit. Raymond and his men turned on them at the gates of his stockade and with elbow room to slaughter he commenced what turned out to be a massacre. He next got his men to stampede the cattle he had stolen. A rush of frightened beasts charged into the packed attackers. The slaughter was extensive, deliberate and systematic. Raymond's small band put to the sword in that panic over 500 until they ceased striking from sheer exhaustion. They then threw stragglers over the cliffs into the sea. Not content with that they arranged an atrocity to impose terror on any other potential attacker.

It was not enough to have felled or captured the pride of

Waterford. From their own side FitzStephen's nephew reports 'they abused their good fortune by evil and detestable counsels and inhuman cruelty, for having gained the victory they kept seventy of the principal townsmen [of Waterford] prisoners in the camp, for whose ransom they might have obtained the city itself or an immense sum of money'. Harvey de Monte Marisco and Raymond took opposite sides of the question during the deliberations. Harvey boldly declared 'of two things we must make choice of one. We must either resolutely accomplish what we have undertaken and stifling all emotions of pity utterly subjugate this turbulent nation by the strong hand and the power of our arms, or yielding to indulging in deeds of mercy as Raymond proposes, set sail homewards and leave both the country and patrimony to this miserable people.' Harvey's opinion was approved by his comrades. The captives, as men condemned, had their legs broken and were thrown over the cliff into the Atlantic.

The interesting thing about this report by FitzStephen's nephew, Cambrensis,[5] is that no respect is paid to Harvey de Monte Marisco or his nephew, Strongbow, throughout. The heroes on the other hand are Nesta's brood. Harvey's speech above is, therefore, composed and put into his mouth by an enemy – although it contained the substance of what Harvey meant to convey. The most menacing repercussion was the evidence that Strongbow's agent, Harvey de Monte Marisco, did not look upon the enterprise in Ireland as merely a hired expedition to help a king. They had determined upon a campaign of acquisition for themselves. And their deed showed that they certainly expected the prompt arrival of reinforcements.

Mac Murchada, who had whetted their appetite with promises, knew too that Strongbow and his faction were in the expedition for land, but he knew they could be controlled, and he knew well that the possibility that Strongbow could succeed him as king of Leinster was out of the question. That was why he promised it.

Raymond le Gros was left, isolated, to sweat it out at Baginbun for three summer months while waiting for Strongbow to follow him.

Mac Murchada must have been disturbed by the atrocity at Dun Donnell. Not only that, but he must have been disillusioned with the poverty of numbers sent for so great a task. He left Raymond le Gros' band to fight their corner alone. Not one handful of men was sent to relieve or encourage him. And the vital three summer months of Mac Murchada's thrust for power were squandered.

Strongbow's preparations for embarkation were only completed by the middle of August 1170.[6] When all had been arranged and the small fleet, loaded with men and material, stood ready to sail from Milford Haven there thundered into the port messengers from Henry II with instructions for Strongbow. Whatever Henry had learned, his orders were unambiguous. Strongbow was forbidden to assemble the expedition, or to launch it to Ireland.[7] This was a calamitous blow to the Mac Murchada enterprise. Strongbow at once took a step that was tantamount to high treason, if that, in fact, is not the definition of what he did. He deliberately disobeyed the orders from his sovereign and set sail for the chosen landing as close as possible to Waterford. Strongbow had burnt his boats long ago. Now he burnt the very timber that might construct a raft. There was nowhere to go now but forward.

On 23 August, 1170 his contingent disembarked at Passage near the confluence of the Suir, the Nore and the Barrow rivers.[8] Amongst the 200 Norman knights and 1,000 others of all ranks and military professions, there was an unexpected inclusion. Strongbow had succeeded in persuading de Prendergast and his Flemish contingent to rejoin the Irish adventure. And that took some persuasion to accomplish. It was an unexpected recruitment which needs study. Was Strongbow looking ahead to a distant confrontation? Did he require, or was he advised by Harvey de Monte Marisco, that he needed men whose loyalty was neither to Diarmait or Henry but to himself? This recall of de Prendergast was evidence already of factions in the relatively small band of mercenaries.

TWENTY-FOUR

The Norsemen's Atlantic Base

Waterford, the 300-year-old Viking city on a reconnoitred and selected site, had never been taken by storm.[1] It had come to arrangements with Diarmait Mac Murchada on two occasions, but devastation had been avoided and commerce had continued. It was the second most important port for commerce and communications in the country. After mourning the deaths of seventy of its citizens at Baginbun, Waterford now heard of the arrival of Strongbow's men. In light of the atrocity committed on their men when prisoners, Waterford decided that whether they were to be starved out or stormed, whether the forces arraigned against them were overwhelmingly superior, whether it would be politic to acknowledge the foe as overlord, whatever the conditions, this time they would fight to the last man and the last house. And so it was.

Two days after the landing Raymond le Gros' relieved contingent loosened their limbs for the first time in three months in open country. They joined Strongbow's forces before the walls of Waterford on 25 August.[2] Their united force, less than 1,300 mercenaries, was hurled upon those walls without delay and was repulsed with zeal. Of Mac Murchada there was no sign. Whatever significance can be deduced from his absence it is out of the question that he did not know of his mercenaries' arrival. The Normans regrouped and positioned themselves for another assault. They threw themselves upon the walls of Waterford for the second time. Again the defenders hurled them back. After this second reverse Raymond le Gros took time to consider. He decided to investigate the Norse fortifications for a weak link. He found it. He discovered a little house of timber standing upon a timber post outside the walls, to which it also hung. He forced on his men from all quarters to renew the assault. This they did and diverted the defenders' attention from their only frail link. He then rushed in men in armour to hack down the support post. When the post eventually came down the house fell and with it came a piece of the wall as well.

Through the dust and masonry Raymond's men raced into the streets slaughtering everything that moved. They killed so efficiently that corpses piled up in the thoroughfares. Among the defenders was Ua Fáeláin, ruler of Déise south west of Waterford.[3] He and a handful of Vikings made a last stand at the Reginald's tower but ultimately they surrendered. Two of the Norse leaders named Sitric were put to the sword in the place they so gallantly defended. The Norse leader, Ragnall, and the Déise ruler Ua Fáeláin were kept for ultimate dispatch.

From devastated Waterford Strongbow sent messengers to Mac Murchada in Ferns announcing the capture of the city. It was at this point only that Diarmait Mac Murchada, with the Norman-Welsh kinsmen, FitzStephen and FitzGerald, marched his men to meet his hired allies. It was the first time he had met the new force, the advance guard of which had been on the soil of his kingdom for three and a half months. Straight away Mac Murchada reprieved the captives, Ragnall and Ua Fáeláin.

Diarmait had his young daughter Aífe with him.[4] The marriage between Aífe, the daughter of Diarmait Mac Murchada and Mór, the daughter of Muirchertach Ua Tuathail, king of Uí Muíredaig, to the earl of Striguil, Strongbow, a man old enough to be her grandfather, has been variously recounted. It has inspired many and famous artistic creations, descriptions, narrative and allegoric verses. The event has incited groans from the Gael and has beaten frowns onto the brows of patriarchs. However, when all is said and done, it must be conceded that no hint or evidence of discontent ever after emerged. There was no repudiation according to Brehon law. There was no recorded realignment on either part afterwards.

For this marriage, however, innovative perceptions were created and developed. While marriages between Irish ruling families and Norse, Welsh and Norman aristocrats were the norm, this marriage was later presented as symbolising a fusion of two foreign cultures, and a fusion moreover made under duress. There is no doubt that the one had a tradition, a culture, a world outlook, an organisation and a legal framework, different to the other. It was the efforts to diminish and misrepresent the differences in the two worlds, the Gaelic world and the feudal world, that gave stimulus to hatred long after the absorption of the Normans.

Mac Murchada now had a new son-in-law, but this one was different. He was Mac Murchada's own age group. Gerald de Barry, who certainly did not smother him in praise, said that he was a man of great generosity and courteous manner. 'What he failed of accomplishing by force he succeeded in by gentle words. In times of peace he was more disposed to be led by others than to command. Out of the camp he had more the air of an ordinary man-at-arms than of a general-in-chief; but in action the mere soldier was forgotten in the commander. With the advice of those about him he was ready to dare anything, but he never ordered any attack relying on his own judgement, or rashly presuming on his personal courage. The post he occupied in battle was a sure rallying point for his troops.' Diarmait had estimated the character of Gerald de Barry before, so he knew the extent of the speech he had held back. It would be premature to dwell on the fact that Strongbow's wife was of the Mac Murchada line with the Mac Murchada instinct and ambition and, indeed, trained by the best Mac Murchada of them all. All conjecture, for major battles, grave days, lay ahead in the immediate future.

The council of war to plan achieving the kingship of Ireland for Mac Murchada assembled in Waterford.[5] The leaders of the combined forces took part: that is, Diarmait's immediate Irish staff, his year-long comrades FitzStephen and FitzGerald, and Strongbow's command which included Raymond le Gros.

Mac Murchada declared Dublin as the next citadel for occupation. Nominal submission with hostages was no longer adequate. On too many occasions the Dublin Norsemen had abruptly changed their allegiance. Possession, the actual physical possession of Dublin, was the next step. It was even conceivable that the city might open its gates without a blood bath. Diarmait's brother-in-law was inside Dublin, for he, Lorcán Ua Tuathail, was the highly regarded archbishop.

A garrison was placed in Waterford, an increasing feature in Irish military security. The army which afterwards marched on Dublin in mid-September was the most diverse force to undertake an Irish operation. The bulk were of Diarmait's Irish. Then there were Strongbow's men who, like himself, were in many cases of the Norman-French race. There were the Flemish, the Welsh, the leaders of Norman-Welsh blood, and lastly the Norse with no other insurance for their security but to fight for Mac Murchada. The formation of Mac Murchada's army as it marched with banners and shields, coats of mail and Irish jerkins, provided variety enough to excite the interest of any observer.

The Norman Milo de Cogan commanded the vanguard with a force estimated at 700 men. He was accompanied by Diarmait's son, Domnall Cáemánach Mac Murchada, with his own troops. The next in line was Raymond le Gros with 800 of the new mercenaries who landed from Wales. He was followed by the man who mounted the entire campaign, Diarmait Mac Murchada, who was surrounded by 1,000 of his own best. Behind Diarmait's division came Strongbow, and in the rear marched an array of Leinstermen.

The intelligence service provided to the Norsemen of Dublin was prompt. They had been informed of the Mac Murchada attack well in advance and had taken precautions. Mac Murchada, in turn, had been informed not alone of the alarm of the Dublin Norsemen but also the position and placing of the troops defending the city. In this regard it was fortuitous that the ruler of the territory immediately south east of Dublin was his son-in-law, Domnall Mac Gilla Mo Cholmóc. His wife's family, the Ua Tuathail, were south of Dublin at modern Powerscourt and his first cousins the Ua Bráenáin were to the south-west around Maynooth.

What had the Norse done? Askulv, their king, had advised the high king of the danger and invoked his aid to the defence of Dublin.[6] Ruaidrí Ua Conchobair, the high king, now assembled his forces for a final dismissal of Mac Murchada. They included Bréifne's Tigernán Ua Ruairc whose regret was that he had never mutilated Mac Murchada. There were the ruler and forces of Meath, and the new Ua Cerbaill ruler of Airgialla. Their forces now infested the main route from the south to Dublin through the woods and also the more difficult passes.

These were the obvious roads which Diarmait would take. Ruaidrí's main force lay in Clondalkin, five miles south-west of Dublin. Mac Murchada had flagrantly broken the terms of their agreement, however, although Ruaidrí was prepared to lead an overwhelmingly superior force against him, he had not harmed a hair on the head of any of Diarmait's hostages.

Mac Murchada, armed with information on the position of his opponents, chose a different route to that expected. He led his army not through the main roads but by the ridges of the mountains overhanging Ua Tuathail's Glendalough. An unconsidered apparition now materialised before the Dublin Norsemen. It was the full extent of Mac Murchada's army in battle formation, having marched to the city over the heights and without one casualty to show for it. The Norsemen decided to accept the inevitable, and through the powerful mediation of Lorcán, archbishop of Dublin, a truce was agreed by the archbishop's brother-in-law, Diarmait Mac Murchada. The truce was to be used to discuss a new and permanent arrangement. Mac Murchada gained another triumph through negotiation. The man in charge of the negotiations on his behalf was his secretary, Maurice Ó Regan. His instructions were simple. Dublin was to be Mac Murchada's and Dublin was to give him thirty of its sons as hostages who would lose their lives the next time it ceased to be his.

The armies which had been assembled to do battle with the Leinstermen and their new auxiliaries quickly identified Mac Murchada's 'ruse de guerre'. When they recovered their wits they turned to face their adversary but discovered that the Dublin

Norsemen had already started negotiations.[7] Since the Norse had taken their own course, Ruaidrí Ua Conchobair considered that his massive donation to Dublin and his assembling had been an utter waste. With angry resignation, crying a plague upon them he left them to their fate. He withdrew his army which had outnumbered Mac Murchada's many times.

Mac Murchada could scarcely believe that the thousands had left the most powerful port and fortress in Ireland for his cleaving. Their withdrawal left the Norse with no hand to play at all. However was that all that could be read into it? Ruaidrí Ua Conchobair, the king of Ireland, with vastly superior numbers, had retreated from *him*. Diarmait Mac Murchada! Ambition, already well fuelled, raced through his veins. It was staring him in the face, the power of Ireland, invitingly placed and if he judged his man correctly that, too, might be achieved without a battle – just a simple statement of submission by Ruaidrí was all that was required. As for Bréifne, and all territories north of Dublin, an injection of punitive violence would throw them into his confederation.

Kings nevertheless have captains and Mac Murchada's authority, even while musing his next and concluding confrontation, was disregarded by two of them. The length of the negotiations was extended by the Norsemen over three days when, in fact, their cause was lost. Mac Murchada did not force the issue by attacking, but this could no longer be endured by Raymond le Gros or Milo de Cogan. They were posted on guard at opposite sides of the city walls.

Suddenly, without warning to the truce-bound Norse or Irish, these two, with their contingents, scaled the walls, opened the gates, and commenced battle.[8] The Norse made no defence, had no defence. The one thing that saved their army, and a great proportion of their citizens, was that their fleet was always riding anchor for such an event. Theirs was a long established ghetto life, and fast, orderly retreat to the sea was a principle basic to their existence.

Many of the Norsemen were slaughtered. Askulv, however, and a considerable concourse of people with their treasures had succeeded in reaching the fleet and escaping. They sailed out of Dublin Bay for the Norse ports in the Isle of Man and the Hebrides, determined on one point, that they had lost the first round only. Nevertheless it was, although they didn't know it at the time, the death of great Viking Dublin after 300 years of commercial dominance and political power, of international development, of living on their finely honed wits in a foreign land where the Gaelic inhabitants outnumbered them many times over.

Mac Murchada now had evidence of what his new armies were capable of. They were not men to be sensitive to conventions like truces or prisoners of war or tossing large numbers of prisoners into the sea – after first breaking their legs. These were men who could easily, if they were given half an inch, round on him, provided he was fool enough not to break their backs with hardship beforehand, but they were required to complete the job. He overlooked their assault on Dublin, for if he had any pity at all it was quenched by the contempt paid by the Dublin Norsemen to his father's dead body. Diarmait turned his thoughts to civil affairs and organisation in the city. He and Strongbow gave their attention to these matters for a few days. Milo de Cogan, was appointed constable.[9] To Mac Murchada it was merely the substitution of one set of foreigners for another. Diarmait then settled on the scourge from Bréifne, Tigernán Ua Ruairc, and the enemies who supported him in Meath and Airgialla. It was not to be a predatory excursion this time, but a carefully executed manoeuvre designed to loosen the mortar supporting the high king. It was designed to be the last but one of the struggles for ultimate power. The last battle – indeed if it went to that – would be with Ruaidrí Ua Conchobair himself.

Mac Murchada led his last campaign to the north of Dublin. They brought punishment with them. He swept through the territories where in his youth he knew friendship and comradeship which had now vanished after four decades of a vacillating life of glory and humiliation. He battered through east Meath, Derbforgaill's and the Ua Máel Sechlainn homeland. He cut apart Clonard and burned Kells to the ground. He foraged through the most sacred and eminent sites in Gaelic history in the valleys of the Boyne and the Blackwater.[10] They then descended upon Tigernán Ua Ruairc's Bréifne, penetrated as far as Slieve Gory and ransacked what wealth they could. Mac Murchada had no pity or restraint for this man. Many prisoners were taken back and many cows, but Tigernán Ua Ruairc escaped the net.[11] It was a costly omission.

Domnall Bregach, king of Meath, who had assassinated his uncle, now brought the kingdom of Meath back into 'Mac Murchada's house', recognised him as overlord and gave him hostages.[12] This withdrawal of allegiance from the high king and Tigernán Ua Ruairc cost the new ruler of Meath the hostages he had with them. The effects of the Mac Murchada combined force produced an even more dramatic acquisition than Meath. In addition to that new and valuable Meath alliance there was added a more powerful one, one which Diarmait Mac Murchada had never achieved before. The Ua Cerbaill and the people of Airgialla had seen and endured enough. They, too, gave hostages to Mac Murchada and 'joined him in the destruction of Tigernán Ua Ruairc'.[13]

Mac Murchada was in control of three-quarters of Ireland.

TWENTY-FIVE

A Corpse for a King

What was Diarmait now to do about Ruaidrí Ua Conchobair?
What of the hostages whom Diarmait loved and who were with
the high king?

For the first time in his reign Ruaidrí was surrounded and
isolated. Despite the fact that Mac Murchada had treated their
agreement with contempt, he still did no harm to his three hostages.
Conchobar, Diarmait's son, promised to Ruaidrí's daughter, had
been singled out by the Irish annalist for an unusual character study.
He was regarded as 'the noblest, and the most amiable youth in
Leinster'. Proud of him as Mac Murchada was, he was also bound
to the two other hostages in bonds of affection. His grandson,
the son of Domnall Cáemánach Mac Murchada, was the first
grandson, the second generation to bear his blood; and Domnall
Cáemánach Mac Murchada himself was very dear to him. Then
there was the son of his foster brother, Diarmait Ua Cáellaide, a
relationship which Mac Murchada could never sufficiently reward.
He was constantly in his days of power bolstering the Ua Cáellaide
interests. The rearing Diarmait had as a foster son must have been
remarkable indeed for he never forgot his foster parents and one
of the most telling evidences of his affection for them was, indeed,
provided when the high king deemed his foster brother's son as
sufficient hostage for Diarmait Mac Murchada's loyalty. Mac
Murchada was certain all the time that Ruaidrí would do his son
and his fellow hostages no harm. And again he had judged Ruaidrí
with accuracy.

Mac Murchada was pushing on in years. The previous four
years in which he had been hurtled from power, then rose from his
knees to conquer again, had punished his physique very severely.
His body had a harsh master, for Mac Murchada had iron will and
grim determination to push himself onwards. He had something

else too, a spur of which there is no sharper to propel any man, namely, the memory of past disgrace, of defeat, of humiliation, of poverty.

Ruaidrí Ua Conchobair had reached the last juncture and he had, in fact, allowed himself to be outmanoeuvred. Now in the eleventh hour he was reluctantly compelled to accept that far from having Diarmait Mac Murchada as a vassal king or ally, what he had now before him was an implacable enemy, an enemy who had his own removal as the next priority. Tigernán Ua Ruairc was bitterly declaring this at the high king's side. Before confrontation took place, Ruaidri decided to act as the high king. He sent Mac Murchada a final ultimatum:[1]

> Contrary to the conditions of our treaty of peace, you have invited a host of foreigners into this island, and yet as long as you kept within the bounds of Leinster we bore it patiently. But now, forasmuch as, regardless of your solemn oaths, and having no concern for the fate of the hostage you gave, you have broken the bounds agreed on, and insolently crossed the frontiers of your own territory. Either restrain in future the irruptions of your foreign bands or we will certainly have your son's head cut off and we will send it to you.

If that last sentence is read carefully it can be said that it provided an opening for Mac Murchada to curb his blatant military antagonism. Mac Murchada did not read it as such. His reading of it was that the high king was bleating too late and bleating from a position of obvious weakness. As for his son, he again correctly estimated that Ruaidrí would not harm him. For if he did, he knew, and Ruaidrí foresaw, that there would not be a hovel, let alone a castle, in Connaught without a dead or mutilated occupant – and that is without contemplating Ruaidrí's personal fate.

Mac Murchada now considered himself as high king – with opposition. He replied to Ruaidrí as such, and his reply, calculated to instil fear in him was as an open-handed slap in the face to Ireland's *de facto* high king.

We will not desist from the enterprise we have undertaken until we have reduced Connaught to subjection, which we claim as our ancient inheritance, and until we have obtained with it the monarchy of the whole of Ireland.

From the evidence Diarmait had seen and from his estimation of Ruaidrí Ua Conchobair, the Leinster leader expected that this reply alone might have settled the issue. He had made no mention of the hostages, thereby indicating to Ruaidrí that he did not consider them worth talking about. They were irrelevant. He had once more reckoned on the absence of the killing instinct in Ruaidrí where, he, Mac Murchada, was involved.

However he had not reckoned on a human being who had these qualities: Tigernán Ua Ruairc, the man whose hatred of Mac Murchada was a growing malignance, the man who would have enjoyed burning a Mac Murchada – any Mac Murchada – alive, the man who with his Bréifne men had preferred slow extinction to acknowledging a Mac Murchada as overlord, and the man who was now the last battle prop of Ruaidrí Ua Conchobair.

Ruaidrí Ua Conchobair was told by Tigernán Ua Ruairc on the receipt of Mac Murchada's arrogant reply to cut the hostages down, for Tigernán Ua Ruairc knew Mac Murchada's weakness. No one in Ireland knew the Mac Murchada weaknesses better, and what he suspected could be confirmed by his wife, Derbforgaill. Ua Ruairc knew that to kill Diarmait Mac Murchada and Mór Ua Tuathail's son, Conchobar, was the last and only way to destroy Mac Murchada, and the more savage the better. The sight of his fine son dismembered and delivered dead in a sack like a bullock for the market place was the one and only halt that would dispatch Mac Murchada, the king of Leinster and the Norse.

Ua Ruairc had reached his most desperate hour. Defeated, with Bréifne in ruins and facing ultimate dispatch he urged the one thing that would cut Mac Murchada down. He demanded death for Conchobar and the other two hostages. Ruaidrí Ua Conchobair refused, but Tigernán was made of sterner stuff and he knew his logistics of power. His reply to Ruaidrí Ua Conchobair's refusal was such that if it was ignored it meant the end of the Ua Conchobair dynasty as a sovereign ruling force. Tigernán Ó Ruairc 'pledged his conscience that Ruaidrí Ua Conchobair would not remain king of Ireland unless the hostages were put to death'.[2]

The Shannon river meanders through Athlone. In that even and placid zone dramatic phases of scholarship, religion, learning and confrontation have been exercised within sight and sound of one another. Clonmacnoise, the university city, aged and glorious, is a small journey down the river. Athlone itself grew around the most vital ford in Ireland and had more blood spilled over its bridges than any other engineering structure. The surrounding countryside is pleasant, calm, not heroic. There are reeds, watercress, bog cotton, rushes and the hoofmarks cattle make in soft soil. The low green banks of the lazy river reduce the haste in men's minds. To this pleasant spot were led the three hostages of Diarmait Mac Murchada. As they faced towards their homelands across the river for the last time they may well have shouted that their executioners would pay a heavy price, but that was all they could do. Shout. A year of pleasant idleness in the Ua Conchobair household was reduced to the obscenity of the execution mound.[3]

The three hostages were beheaded and their bodies were sent to Diarmait Mac Murchada, father of one, grandfather of another, foster uncle of the third.

TWENTY-SIX

The Death of Diarmait the King

Diarmait Mac Murchada started to die.[1] For him from that time all other matters were left to progress of their own volition. The movements he had set in motion spluttered spasmodically. The vigorous world, which carries on with unabated and perpetual motion no matter how calamitous a death, passed him by.

The son upon whom he had set much store, the son of ruling potential, whose inheritance was of glittering promise, was now a dismembered corpse, cut down as surely as if Mac Murchada himself had wielded the battleaxe. Mac Murchada had gambled with the lives of his own. He had miscalculated with egotistical zeal and grievously he had lost. What was honour but a brief tenure of that quality, with the contentment of being able to lend it to someone who is loved at the end of one's life?

It was winter when the broken king left the grim mediaeval city of Dublin for the last time. He was going to Ferns for the winter months to face the grief of Mór, his wife and queen, his son, Domnall Cáemánach Mac Murchada and his aged foster brother Diarmait Ua Cáellaide; the grief, the blame of broken-hearted mothers and wives. There is nothing as final as death; there is no death more abrupt than an execution. Mac Murchada himself was the creator of the anguish.

The world's nonsense continued. The clergy held another synod at Armagh. Petrified with the events of the year, they deliberated long and exhaustively on the arrival of Mac Murchada's mercenaries as if they had never heard the like before. It was unanimously resolved 'that it appeared to the synod that the divine vengeance had brought upon them this severe punishment for the sins of the people and especially for this, that they had long been wont to purchase natives of England, as well from traders as from robbers and pirates, and reduce them to slavery'.[2] It mattered little to

Mac Murchada. That winter he disappeared from the stadium of history.

Of his reaction to the winter months' events there is no hint or record. There is only silence, the more eloquent for the fact that he was now being ignored. There was one last dramatic development at the close of his life but in which he had neither participation nor negotiation. Much exaggerated reports of Mac Murchada's campaign had reached Henry II.[3] Henry's reaction was sharp. He issued a proclamation which stated that in future 'no ship sailing from any part of his dominions should carry anything to Ireland and that all his subjects who had been at any time conveyed there should return before the following Easter on pain of forfeiting their lands and being banished from Henry's kingdom forever.'

This roar of discontent with the entire Norman mercenary force put Strongbow into instant retreat, but he regrouped and launched a flattering letter to Henry which was carried over by Raymond le Gros to Aquitaine in France.

My lord and king, it was with your licence, as I understood, that I came over to Ireland for the purpose of helping your faithful liegeman Diarmait in the recovery of his lands. Whatever lands therefore I have had the good fortune to acquire in this country, either in right of Diarmait's patrimony, or from any other person, I consider to be owing to your gracious favour and I shall hold them at your free disposal.

Raymond was received coldly but, nevertheless, Henry deferred judgement on Strongbow.

The condition of the king who hired Strongbow deteriorated. By April of 1171 he was in serious disintegration. When it became apparent that Diarmait Mac Donnchada Mac Murchada would not live, his three sons-in-law were added to the waiting family at Ferns. They were three remarkable men of interest and contrast in any country's story. There was Domnall Mór Ua Briain, king of Munster's Thomond, successor of Brian Bóruma. There was the ruler of Cuala, Domnall Mac Gilla Mo Cholmóc, and there was his latest son-in-law, the Norman's senior commander, Strongbow, who had rushed from Dublin to be at the seat of power when power became available.[4]

Diarmait Mac Murchada, king of Leinster and the Norse, lived until the first day of May 1171, when at last the turbulent light of his life was quenched. The notice of his passing is recorded in the *Book of Leinster*, compiled late in the twelfth century and which remains today one of the glories of Gaelic civilisation. It is recorded without any of the barbed malignance quoted at the beginning of our work:

> *Diarmait Mac Donnchada Mac Murchada reigned for forty-six years. And he was king of all southern Ireland and also of Meath. He died at Ferns after the victory of Extreme Unction and Penance in the sixty-first year of his age.*

And so Diarmait Mac Murchada left this life for another tribunal. He died conscious of personal disaster.

In the minds of his countrymen today not more than five pre-Norman monarchs are household words. Niall Noígiallach, Conchobar Mac Nessa, Brian Bóruma, Ruaidrí Ua Conchobair. These names are gilded in heroism. The name of Diarmait Mac Murchada is swathed in infamy. In the wretchedness of his last days this consideration would not have overwhelmed him. He was better dead. Yet he was to fill a function the provision of which is a prerequisite of every nation. From the time of his death to this day, he, personally, has become the scapegoat for Ireland's defeats.

The cross with the broken shaft to be seen in the graveyard of the ancient cathedral of Ferns marks the site of the grave where Diarmait Mac Murchada's body was laid to rest. It is of late Celtic workmanship but bears no inscription now. It is constructed of granite. Covered all over this enduring stone is a strange pattern known to the students of archaeology as the 'key pattern' or 'Greek Fret'. Yet an ingenuity has been displayed on Diarmait Mac Murchada's tombstone.[5] The simple 'key pattern' was so altered by the craftsman who made it that while its identification as the 'key pattern' is beyond controversy, nevertheless each side of the shaft that marks the last resting place of Diarmait displays a different design. The mind which guided the hands knew the man who was to be commemorated.

TWENTY-SEVEN

The Aftermath of Diarmait

In accordance with Brehon law, as Mac Murchada had known when he was alive, there was an election held to select his successor.

The regnal list in the *Book of Leinster* records that the men who succeeded Diarmait Mac Murchada as king of Uí Chennselaig were Murchad Mac Donnchada Mac Murchada, Domnall Cáemánach Mac Diarmait Mac Murchada who is also listed as ruler over the men of Leinster and Muirchertach Mac Murchada Mac Murchada. The first-named was Diarmait's brother who ruled while Diarmait was in exile. The second-named is that of his own son, Domnall Cáemánach Mac Murchada, and the last-named is the son of Diarmait's brother, Murchad.[1] Within a relatively short space of time Muirchertach became king of Uí Chennselaig.

Strongbow was not considered, nor could he be as only those of Mac Murchada royal blood were eligible for election as king. No matter what high sounding bribes Diarmait Mac Murchada had offered, the concept that the ambitious Mac Murchada contestants or their followers would or could elect as king a total outsider and military mercenary like Strongbow without a drop of inherited Irish royal blood in his veins is ludicrous. There was rage undoubtedly in the deceived Strongbow but by August in that year he made peace with the new king and, in fact, spent days in Ferns castle.[2] The ancient Gaelic Brehon kingdom and kingdoms continued. Gaelic Ireland, despite the turbulence of the next years, had seen far worse, and if the Norsemen were a minority the Normans were much more so, albeit extremely effective fighting animals. Twelfth-century Gaelic Ireland lived with the memory of fierce Norse raids, raids which had penetrated as far as Roscrea and in Uí Chennselaig alone had destroyed Ferns in addition to the records and relics of two great monastic settlements, Begerin and Taghmon.

Ruaidrí Ua Conchobair, the last clearly acknowledged king of Ireland, lived until 1198, a retired king.[3] In October 1175 Ruaidri made the Treaty of Windsor with Henry II by which he recognised Henry as lord, and Henry recognised Ruaidrí as high king of Gaelic Ireland. In the Irish concept and norm it would be accepted as an arrangement of convenience, certainly without permanence and definitely dependant on the prevailing circumstances. It was by no means a feudal absorption. Derbforgaill the widow of Ua Ruairc, died in 1193, aged eighty-five years, in the convent she herself had endowed at Mellifont and to which she had retired.[4]

Tigernán Ua Ruairc survived Mac Murchada by one year.[5] However, as Mac Murchada lay dying in Ferns, Tigernán Ua Ruairc celebrated by several raids into east Meath, captured numerous cattle and 'the dog of war burned the round tower of Tullyard with its full of human beings'. There followed a clash between Ua Ruairc and the Norman, de Lacy, in Meath. His last foray is described in the *Annals of Ulster*.

Tigernán Ua Ruairc, king of Bréifne and Conmaicne, a man of great power for a long time, was killed by the Saxons, and by Domnall, son of Annadh Ua Ruairc of his own clan, along with them. He was beheaded also by them, and his head and body were carried ignominiously to Dublin. The head was raised over the gate of the fortress, a sore miserable sight for the Gael. The body was hung in another place with the feet upwards.

This last barbarism in Ua Ruairc's life story was without parallel in the period on Norse, Welsh, Norman-French or Irish sides. One can interpret the insult to a slain enemy's corpse as evidence that the thirst to revenge Diarmait Mac Murchada's misery had survived. If any of the Normans had been favoured with Mac Murchada's intimacy, or indeed if Aífe had told Strongbow anything of her father's life, then the details of his long and bitter enmity with Ua Ruairc culminating in the slaying of his son, grandson, and foster nephew as hostages, would have been widely known. Diarmait's foster brother, Ua Cáellaide, the father of the slain hostage, died in this year also as the wars, strifes and raids continued.[6]

The girl who might have proved a suitable wife to the slain Conchobar Mac Murchada, Rós Ua Conchobair, daughter of the high king Ruaidrí Ua Conchobair, was sought and won by one of the most successful of the Normans, Hugh de Lacy, the man who had a hand in Tigernán Ua Ruairc's dispatch.[7] Diarmait Mac Murchada's granddaughter, the daughter of Domnall Mór Ua Briain, king of Thomond, married another Norman commander, William de Burgh.[8]

There are questions which remain unanswered. The first question is what became of Mac Murchada's principal wife, Mór Ua Tuathail, to whom he was certainly canonically married or of the first wife he took, Sadb Ua Fáeláin? Or the other women in his life? What were their relationships to one another? What was the conclusion of their story? To all of these questions no certain answer is possible. The Irish annalists rarely go into details about women. What was abnormal was recorded, namely, the deliberate breaking of the Brehon law by one sworn to uphold it, as in Diarmait's possession of Derbforgaill without the payment of the legislated honour price to her husband the king of Bréifne.

Mac Murchada's sons-in-law went their separate ways once the great influence was entombed. Domnall Mór Ua Briain of Thomond used the Normans at his whim – as did every other Irish sovereign.[9] He hired them, helped them, and inflicted flight on them at will. They were still only a small force of efficient mercenaries not 2,000 in number.

Mac Murchada's third son-in-law, Strongbow, French-Norman by race, ended his days an elderly fighting bear with scarcely time to rest until he lay on his death bed. When not involved in Ireland, he was summoned to aid his king abroad. If he was disillusioned he showed little sign of it and contemporary appraisals acknowledge in him the qualities of statesman rather than warrior, but he was doomed to the camp and the saddle in the evening of his life. On Mac Murchada's death when he might have thought of succession he was befriended by only Domnall Cáemánach Mac

Murchada and two other minor Irish dynasts.[10] By the end of 1171 Strongbow was without title or official position save that of chief of hired men.[11] He was compelled from beleaguered Dublin to offer to become the 'man' of the high king, Ruaidrí Ua Conchobair, and 'to hold Leinster from him'. At the year's end he had simply replaced the Norse as the senior officer of the occupants of their land at Dublin, Wexford and Waterford, plus grants of land along the Atlantic coast of Leinster between Wexford and Waterford.[12]

The man Strongbow feared was his king, Henry, and Henry regarded Strongbow with suspicion.[13] What Henry feared was a rival Norman king in Ireland. Strongbow dispatched his uncle, Harvey de Monte Marisco who found Henry at Argentan in July of 1171. On Strongbow's behalf, Harvey submitted to Henry the former Viking ports of Wexford, Waterford and Dublin. The king of the Normans offered to restore Strongbow to his former estates in Wales and Normandy, and to appoint him constable of the new acquisitions compulsorily released by the Norsemen in Ireland.

There was, however, another announcement. Henry himself decided personally to come to Ireland. He had been dismayed at Strongbow and the entire Irish enterprise and was anxious to co-operate with the Irish civil and religious authorities in limiting the power of his barons.[14] His sheriff of Gloucestershire had prosecuted and fined the Jewish merchant, Josce, who lent the money which funded the expedition of Robert FitzStephen and Maurice FitzGerald, 'those who against the king's prohibition went over to Ireland'.[15] Undoubtedly, with Diarmait dead it was Henry's only alternative.

Henry's landing force of 4,000 men were fed and fuelled by provisions brought with them, and wine purchased in Waterford.[16] The necessary equipment for all events was taken along. They landed near the Norman-garrisoned port of Waterford. With the significant exception of the high king, Ruaidrí Ua Conchobair, and the northern Irish rulers, the remaining Irish kings made the usual gestures of submission, an annual or indeed biennial ritual with no more permanence attached to it in the Irish context than at any time in the past.[17] As far as the ambitions and rivalries in Ireland were concerned, the Normans were another element who had merely replaced the Norsemen and were not nearly as numerous. The anticipated full-scale invasion did not take place.

Henry was in disgrace with Christendom for the murder of Thomas á Becket, archbishop of Canterbury. He dealt in pious fashion with the Irish hierarchy and with the papal legate, Gilla Críst Ua Connairche, the Cistercian bishop of Lismore, to whom he devoted two days for conference. The papal legate presided at the synod of Cashel requested by Henry and once more regulations were promulgated to normalise, as Rome saw it, the sexual free-for-all of the Brehon law, church organisation, tithes, will-making, the sacraments, last rites and baptism. The influence of Brehon custom was emphasised in clause five which read 'that in compensation for murder by laymen, clergymen, though of kin to the perpetrators, will pay no part of the fine'.

Henry then proceeded to reduce Strongbow to a position of weakness.[18] Strongbow had already surrendered the former Norse enclaves in the kingdom of Leinster to Henry, and he reduced those whom he suspected might have independent notions. Robert FitzStephen was deprived of Wexford and the lands given him by Diarmait Mac Murchada. He spent his future days hacking an estate for himself near Cork. Henry appointed dependable constables in charge of the former Viking ports. Not one of them was a follower of Strongbow.[19] Henry's most antagonistic manoeuvre was his introduction of Hugh de Lacy. This man was granted the chaos of Meath and the command of Dublin as a block to Strongbow. The word 'grant' needs interpretation, for with understandable persistence the Ua Máel Sechlainn regarded it as an intrusion which could not be taken seriously. Not only did they continue in their ancestral function but several hundred years later died demonstrating their proper place in the scheme of Irish things.

Two documents issued by Henry II are signed evidence of his visitation.[20] One is the first written charter of Dublin as a city in which Henry replaces the Norse by citizens of Bristol, one of whom was a FitzHarding. The other charter granted a piece of land near the convent founded by Diarmait Mac Murchada, St Mary de Hogges, to a wealthy citizen of Bristol named Adelm.

The king of the Normans, whose story along with Diarmait's has provided such interest over 800 years, left Dublin for the port of Wexford at the beginning of Lent in 1172. He spent the penitential season there doing penance and taking part in all the religious exercises until Easter Sunday. On Easter Monday morning he sailed at sunrise from Wexford to face at last the stern representatives of the man who made and unmade kings, the pope. He landed in Wales at noon on the same day and never laid eyes on Ireland again.

The nineteenth-century historian of Ireland under the Normans, Goddard Orpen, has one shaft of understanding Henry II's visit. He concludes his appraisal of Henry's diplomacy:

> *Appearances were deceptive. Henry was really far from having secured his own dominance over the kings who had so readily submitted to him, or an effective control over the lords to whom he had granted large fiefs. To the Irish kings their acknowledgement of Henry as overlord meant no more than the similar acknowledgement which they had often given, and broken, to the ard rí. No, as Henry would be far off across the seas, they probably expected it to mean a great deal less.*

Strongbow, never free of suspicion, was worked like an even-tempered cart horse. Despite his years, Henry felt he would be safer at his side. So the battered knight now approaching his mid-sixties was dragooned to fight another campaign in France.[21] The veteran acquitted himself so well that at life's end he won his way into the scarce esteem of Henry and was given leave to return to Ireland and custody of the former Viking possessions. Strongbow returned to all the familiar ingredients, to which alongside Norsemen and Irish kings were now joined the Norman freebooters.

Strongbow is perceived by many as a powerful autocrat. His

wife was never given equal status, despite being the daughter of Diarmait with all the mental agility, long-term endurance, ambition and blood of the Mac Murchadas. When he died in 1176 his only son, Gilbert, was a minor who died shortly after 1185 – before coming of age. Aífe and Strongbow had a daughter, Isabella, who became their sole remaining heir. Isabella, Diarmait Mac Murchada's granddaughter, became one of the most powerful women in Europe. She married William le Marshal, sometime viceroy, lord deputy of Ireland, earl of Pembroke, lord of Leinster. By Isabella's inheritance Marshal also became joint owner of her father's and mother's considerable properties, lands and offices in county Wexford, Leinster, Wales, England and France.

The Norman leaders could see that there were lands and battles to be won. Each Irish ruler viewed them as war specialists for hire. Many preferred to submit to Strongbow rather than to a hated neighbour. The ruler of Osraige did exactly that rather than bow the knee to the new king of Uí Chennselaig, a Mac Murchada. So the Normans became another element in the warring fabric of Ireland. They found a more agreeable civilisation than their own and land worth fighting for. They integrated as a matter of policy and married into the leading Irish families. Once married to an Irish girl they were on an irreversible course of absorption.

The void left by the death of Mac Murchada was never filled. There was no one, not even the high king, Ruaidrí Ua Conchobair, with the imagination or greatness, cunning or personality to play the field or cement the factions. Diarmait and Henry's friend, FitzHarding, had died in 1170 in Bristol. Diarmait's son, Domnall Cáemánach Mac Murchada, the ancestor of the family branch of the same name, was killed by two men of the territory of Uí Nualláin in 1175 while still an able man, perhaps more able than Muirchertach Mac Murchada.[22] Strongbow lived long enough to see Henry II take it upon himself to parcel out Gaelic lands to Normans, or to be more accurate, spheres in which they could, if they were capable, try to hold land.[23] The Norman adventurers were left to fight their corner as individual war lords. The ensuing struggles were for power between mixed groups of mutually vying aristocrats, Gaelic and Norman. No unified plan of conquest was operated.

Church reform was moderately successful, but at terrible cost to those of the Irish race who introduced French discipline. French discipline by Norman prelates in monastic and diocesan rule soon succeeded the Irish, reformers and all, on their own soil. The result was a militant division in the reforming Church which culminated in the strife among the Cistercians, more euphemistically termed the 'conspiracy of Mellifont'.[24] For it was in the Church, as in state, law and politics, a confrontation with a foreign concept, outlook, tradition; two implacably opposing cultures.

And the Brehon law, unrepentant and unconvinced, still obtained in the land. What of Brehon Ireland – or what of Brehon Leinster? Until the sixteenth century the original core of Uí Chennselaig was not encroached upon. The king of Uí Chennselaig continued using the title king of Leinster. Almost 300 years after the time of Diarmait Mac Murchada another Domnall, Domnall Mac Murchada Cáemánach, was king of Uí Chennselaig and king of Leinster.[26] His seal may be examined with his title and coat of arms embossed upon it in Latin: *Sigillum Donati Mac Murchada, Regis Lageie.* In 1570 the hereditary Brehon judge of Uí Chennselaig, Ó Doráin, held office of such acknowledged validity and integrity that officers of the English crown were compelled to consult him on matters of law. The monks and the abbot of the monastery of Glascarraig on the sea coast nearest to Ferns were Gaelic. At the close of the sixteenth century, that is over 400 years after Diarmait Mac Murchada's reign, the following English report of 1599 gives an indication of the situation and emphasises the gulf between the two civilisations. It refers to the Mac Murchada Cáemánach known to us as Donal Spainneach:

> … *Donnel Spaniaghe, whoe now pretends to be chief of the Kavanagh and the Mac Murchada, which in the Irish accompte is noeless than to be kinge of Leinster …*[27]

In Osraige the situation was similar and that story has been told through the industry of William Carrigan. In short, the problems, ambitions, feuds, battles of all the familiar Leinster states continued into the seventeenth century with the name of the ruling family of almost each state remaining the same. There was a reluctant system of coexistence of two different laws and interpretations in one land, with the one system incomprehensible to the upholders of the other.

Ireland was not overwhelmed. Ireland absorbed the Normans and has benefited from their contribution. Reduction first appeared on the horizon for Brehon Ireland in the sixteenth century. With the discovery of the Americas, Ireland, because of its position on the Atlantic ocean route to the new world, became the focus of strategic appetite to imperial and mutually antagonistic powers, England, Spain and France. The possession of Ireland with its harbours on the Atlantic fringe of Europe ensured that control of Ireland's facilities by European kingdoms, consumed by the prospects of immeasurable wealth, was inevitable. The survival of Ireland's old royal families to this day is explained on the one hand by their flights to France, Spain, Austria and Portugal. The old royal families who survived at home did so in many cases by reaching accommodation with the English crown which had achieved control. What was left of Brehon Ireland, and indeed of old Norman Ireland was overthrown by Cromwell between 1649 and 1652. This harsh regime of confiscation, expulsion and plantation, had nevertheless the opposite effect to that intended. It laid the foundation stone of the modern nation.

NOTES

CHAPTER 1: THE INHERITANCE
1. *Wars of the Gael with the Gaill,* R.S. pp. 136–40, 212–16, B. Ó Cuív, *Course of Irish History.* (7). J. Ryan, 'Brian Bóruma'. *North Munster Studies.* F. J. Byrne, *The Rise of the Uí Neill Kingship of Ireland.*
2. *Bardic Poems of Tadgh Dall Ó Huíginn,* Poem 17.
3. *Book of Leinster.* LL 311. A. Ua Cleirig, *History of Ireland,* p. 395.
4. *Book of Ballymote,* (RIA). E. O'Curry, *Ancient Irish History.* L. Ginnell, *The Brehon Laws.* G. H. Orpen, *Ireland Under the Normans,* chap. 4, vol. 1. P. W. Joyce, *Social History of Ancient Ireland. Crith Cablach,* edited by D. A. Binchy. E. MacNeil, *Phase Irish History,* D. A. Gleeson, *History of the Diocese of Killaloe,* Part 2, pp. 152–55. A. Gwynn, 'Twelfth-Century Reform'. *History of Irish Catholicism,* edited by P. J. Corish, pp. 13–19.
5. *Annals of the Four Masters.*
6. E. Campion, *History of Ireland,* Reprint 1809, p. 23.
7. *Sylloge,* edited by J. Usher.
8. M. Richards, 'Irish Settlements South-West Wales'. *RSAI,* vol. XC, pt. 2.
9. *Wars of the Gael with the Gaill.*
10. D. Ó Corráin, 'The Career of Diarmait Mac Máel na mBó', *Journal of the Old Wexford Society,* nos. 3, 4.
11. J. P. Dalton, 'St Vauk of Carne'. *The Past* 1921. P. Murphy, *Our Lady's Island.*
12. G. Hadden, 'Origin and Development of Wexford Town', *Journal of the Old Wexford Society,* nos. 1–3. P. H. Hore, *History of Town and County of Wexford.*
13. *Annals of Ulster,* 1162.
14. P. Walsh, 'Leinster States and Kings'. *Irish Ecclesiastical Record,* 1939, p. 47, *Book of Rights.*

CHAPTER 2: FERNS
1. *Book of Leinster. Genealogies.* Prior to the Norman adventurers, the word Gall or foreigner meant the Danes, Norse, Vikings or Ostmen. The title 'king of Leinster and the foreigners' granted to Diarmait Mac Murchada and those of his predecessors who achieved it can be traced from several Irish manuscript sources. Note pedigree of St Laurence by E. O'Curry in J. O'Hanlon's *Life of the Saint,* p. 12. The Norse settlements in Wexford, Waterford and Dublin owed homage and service to the king of Leinster *(Book of Rights).* It has recently been suggested that the surviving *Book of Rights* is a twelfth-century alteration of the original by Diarmait Mac Murchada. F. J. Byrne, *New History of Ireland,* vol. 2. (Ed. A. Cosgrove) p. 27.
2. P. W. Joyce, *Social History of Ancient Ireland.*
3. ibid.
4. *Annals of Ulster,* N. Furlong, 'The Immediate Predecessors of Dermot Mac Murrough', *Journal of the Old Wexford Society,* no. 4.
5. *Annals of Tig. Annals of Ulster. Book of Leinster,* p. 39 D.
6. *Miscellaneous Irish Annals, The Historical Works of Giraldus Cambrensis.*
7. *Miscellaneous Irish Annals,* 1115.
8. W. Carrigan, *History Diocese of Ossory,* vol. 1, pp. 4, 20.

9. *Book of Leinster*. N. Furlong, 'Immediate Predecessors of Dermot Mac Murrough', *Journal Old Wexford Society*, no. 4.
10. *Annals of Loch Ce.*
11. *Book of Leinster.*
12. *Annals Tig. Annals of Loch Ce. Misc. Ir. Anns.*
13. ibid. *Book of Leinster*, but note D. Ó Corráin, Irish Regnal Succession, no. 11, P. 26. *Studia Hibernica.*
14. P. W. Joyce, *Social History of Ancient Ireland*. I am grateful to Elizabeth Fitzpatrick, NUIG, for allowing me to consult her thesis on Irish Royal Inauguration Sites.

CHAPTER 3: POWER
1. J. Ryan. *Toirdelbach Ua Conchobair.*
2. *Annals of Ulster. Annals of Loch Ce.* ' … but the ill fame of that campaign rested on Tigernán Ua Ruairc'.

CHAPTER 4: THE MAN
1. *Annals of Loch Ce.*
2. *Annals Tig*, 1131.
3. M. T. Flanagan, *Irish Society Anglo-Norman Settlers Angevin Kingship*. p. 101.
4. ibid. P.96
5. *Annals of Ulster*, 1127. *Misc. Ir. Anns.*
6. *Annals of Loch Ce*, 1132. *Annals of Clonmacnoise*, 1135, p. 193.
7. *Annals of Loch Ce.*
8. ibid, 1171.
9. *Four Masters*, 1134.
10. *Annals of Loch Ce.*
11. *Annals of Loch Ce*, 1134. *Annals Tig.*

CHAPTER 5: A FORCE TO BE RECKONED WITH
1. *Annals of Loch Ce. Annals Tig. Misc. Ir. Anns.*
2. *Annals Tig.*
3. *Four Masters*, 1132.
4. *Annals Tig. Annals of Ulster. Four Masters*, 1137. A Ua Cléirigh, *History of Ireland.*
5. ibid. Cormac's chapel on the Rock of Cashel was built by Cormac Mac Carthaig and was consecrated in 1134. G. H. Orpen, *Ireland Under the Normans*, vol. 1, p. 48.
6. *Annals of Clonmacnoise*, 1136.
7. *Four Masters*, 1138.
8. A. Gwynn, 'Twelfth-Century Reform', *History of Irish Catholicism*, edited by Corish.

CHAPTER 6: ALL LEINSTER FAR UNDER HAND
1. *Annals Tig. Four Masters.*
2. ibid.
3. ibid.
4. *Brut Y Tywsogion.*

5. M. T. Flanagan, *op. cit.* p. 96
6. *Annals of the Four Masters.*
7. ibid. *Annals Tig.*
8. *Annals of the Four Masters.*
9. ibid.
10. *Annals Tig. Four Masters.*
11. ibid.
12. ibid.
13. *Chronicum Scotorum. Annals of the Four Masters.*
14. J. F. Shearman, 'Early Kings of Ossory', *Kilkenny Archaeological Journal*, vol. 4, p. 336. *Book of Leinster.* W. Carrigan, *History of the Diocese of Ossory*, vol. 1. p. 55.
15. *Annals Tig.*

CHAPTER 7: UÍ NÉILL SEIZE POWER

1. *Four Masters*, 1147–50.
2. *Four Masters.*
3. ibid.
4. *Annals Tig*, 1151. *Misc. Ir. Anns.*

CHAPTER 8: MAC MURCHADA PRESTIGE

1. Colmcille, *The Story of Melifont.* A. Gwynn & R. N. Hadcock, *Med. Religious Houses.*
2. J. Farrow, *Pageant of the Popes.*
3. Colmcille, *The Story of Mellifont.* A. Gwynn & R. N. Hadcock, *Med. Religious Houses.*
4. Letter from Bernard, abbot of Clairvaux to Malachy, apostolic legate in Ireland, Cod. Nummer 70/291. Fol. 96 V. Nummer 140, Wien. Dominikanerkloster, Konventsbibliothek.

Brother Bernard, so called the abbot of Clairvaux, sends greetings and good wishes to Malachy, that great priest and close friend who is a legate of the apostolic see.

Though you may be separated from us by a long distance, you are very close to our heart, because holy love can overcome the impediments of time and distance. We are separated by an ocean, but united by charity. For charity is certainly implied in the font of affection which neither an ocean nor waters can extinguish and which is not destroyed by fire. In this sense you are always with me and I with you. For otherwise we should not love Christ our Lord and God from whom we seek knowledge for learning, life for the sake of conscience, and instruction for our example.

But above all, what unites me to you is your gracious acceptance of our sons and brothers who have lately journeyed to those parts. These you have cherished and loved and helped to a great extent. For even though they have not come from our own house, spiritually speaking, they are equally beloved of our own brethren since we are all, far and near, united in Christ. These along with the people who have lately come to you from here we commend in a special way to your patronage, praying that you may successfully conclude what you have so happily begun.

And that you may do so more freely, we make you a participant in all the good works which we perform or may perform in our Order for all time.

(The Canons Regular of St Augustine are not to be confused with the Augustinians of today).

5. B. W. O'Dwyer, *The Conspiracy of Mellifont.*
6. A. Gwynn & Hadcock, *Med. Religious Houses,* See J. Ware's *Bishops.*
7. ibid.
8. ibid.
9. Letter from Bernard, Abbot of Clairvaux, to Dermot, King of Ireland. Cod. nummer 70/291. Fol. 96V. Nummer 141. Wien, Dominikanerkloster, Konventsbibliothek.
10. *Pont. Hib.*, 1. 19, no. 5, note 1, edited by M. P. Sheehy.
11. A. Gwynn & R. N. Hadcock, *Med. Religious Houses.*
12. *Annals of the Four Masters,* 1152. S. Ceitinn, *Foras Feasa ar Éirinn.* J. F. O'Doherty, 'St Laurence O'Toole', *IER,* 1937, p. 458. A. Gwynn, 'The Centenary of the Synod of Kells', *IER,* March/April 1952.
13. *Annals Tig., Four Masters, Ulster.*
14. ibid.
15. *Annals of the Four Masters, Tig., Clonmacnoise.*

CHAPTER 9: THE WIFE OF TIGERNÁN UA RUAIRC

1. *Annals Tig.,* 1153. *Four Masters.*
2. *Misc. Ir. Anns.,* Mary T. Flanagan, *Irish Society, Anglo-Norman Settlers,* p.101.
3. ibid. *Annals Tig. Four Masters, Clonmacnoise, Song of Dermot and the Earl.*
4. See Mary T. Flanagan op. cit., p. 102.
5. *Annals Tig,* 1153, *Four Masters.*
6. *Four Masters.*
7. Paul Walsh, Kings of Meath in *IER,* Jan – June, 1941.
8. *Annals Tig, Four Masters.* The son of Eochaidh Ó Nualláin, the hereditary inaugurator of the Mac Murchada kings was killed in this raid.
9. ibid, *Annals of Ulster,* J. Ryan, *Toirdelbach Ua Conchobair.*
10. B. W. O'Dwyer, *The Conspiracy of Mellifont.*

CHAPTER 10: THE WORLD SCENE

1. J. Farrow, *Pageant of the Popes.* A. Ua Cléirigh, *History of Ireland.* M. Kelly, 'Synod of Cashel', *Dissertations on Irish History.* G. T. Stokes, *Ireland and the Anglo-Norman Church.*
2. Bernard, abbot of Clairvaux, letter 361, vol. 182, p. 502, J. P. Migne (ed).
3. John of Salisbury, *Metalogicon,* C. C. J. Webb (ed). ———
4. *Pont Hib.,* Brief Alexander III, vol. 1, 19–20, M. P. Sheehy (ed).

CHAPTER 11: DEATH OF A KING

1. *Annals Tig., Four Masters.* J. Ryan, *Toirdelbach Ua Conchobair.*
2. ibid.
3. *Annals Tig.*
4. *Annals of Ulster,* 1155.
5 W. Carrigan, *History of the Diocese of Ossory.*
6. ibid. A. Gwynn & R. N. Hadcock, *Med. Religious Houses.*
7. P. Walsh, *IER,* 'Kings of Meath', Jan to June 1941.

8. ibid. *Annals Tig., Ulster.*
9. *Annals Ulster, Tig., Four Masters,* 1159.

CHAPTER 12: 'THE MAN WHO IS NOT STRONG ...'
1. In a manuscript of Giraldus Cambrensis *(Wildes Catalogue)* there is a full-length drawing of Diarmait Mac Murchada.
2. D. Ó Corráin, *MSS. Materials of Ancient Irish History.* G. T. Stokes, *Ireland and the Anglo-Norman Church.*
3. P. H. Hore, *History of the Town and County of Wexford.* 'Episcopal list'. Ferns, vol. 6. Edward Culleton, *Celtic Early Christian Wexford*
4. ibid.
5. P. H. Hore, Hook, vol. 3.
6. P. H. Hore, Ferns, vol. 6.
7. *Genealogies.*
8. For protection given the Ua Cáellaide read the *History of the Diocese of Ossory* by W. Carrigan, vol. 1, chap. 6, p. 55. Diarmait's friend, the high king Mac Lochlainn, emphasised Osraige as a dependant state of Leinster. A. Gwynn & R. N. Hadcock, *Med. Religious Houses.* 'Leighlin', p. 89. The bishop who succeeded to the diocese of Leighlin in 1145 was Dungal Ua Caéllaide. This Ua Caéllaide bishop was the second witness to Diarmait's charter of Ferns abbey, after the papal legate, Gilla Críst, bishop of Lismore, and before Seosamh Ua hAeda, Diarmait's bishop of Ferns.
9. G. T. Stokes, *Ireland and the Anglo-Norman Church.* Translation of charter to All Hallows in the lecture 'St Laurence O'Toole'. List of witnesses given by G. T. Stokes is incomplete. They include Mac Murchada's daughter Derbforgaill. See *Registrum Priorat Om. SS.* J. Ware's *Bishops,* T. Harris, (ed) p. 180. Diarmait's son-in-law, Mac Gilla Mo Cholmóc, rídomna of Cuala, married to the above Derbforgaill was another witness, and, of course, Diarmait's foster brother, Aed Ua Cáellaide, bishop of Louth or Clogher. Aed Ua Cáellaide is styled 'bishop of Airgialla' in the Martyrology of Máelmaire Ua Gormain. See *MSS Materials of Ancient Irish History,* Ó Curry.
10. A. Gwynn & R. N. Hadcock, *Med. Religious Houses.*
11. *Annals of Ulster, Tig.*
12. *Annals Tig. Misc. Ir. Anns.*
13. G. T. Stokes, *Ireland and the Anglo-Norman Church,* p. 61. Wm. of Newburg, *Chron, Henry II, t.* 11 pref, pp. 42, 68. *Brut Y Tywysogion,* pp. 201–3.
14. *Annals Tig. Misc. Ir. Anns.*
15. ibid. D. F. Gleeson, *History of the Diocese of Killaloe,* part 2.
16. P. H. Hore, *History of the Town and County of Wexford.* 'Ecclesiastical and Municipal Annals of Ferns', p. 181. *Trias Thaumaturga,* J. Colgan (ed). p. 633. *Annals of the Four Masters,* J. O'Donovan, *Ordnance Survey Letters, County Wexford.* p. 74.

CHAPTER 13: DISASTER
1. *Annals of Ulster,* 1165. For a concise account of the Ulster states and their difference see F. J. Byrne, *Rise of the Uí Neill and the High Kingship of Ireland.*
2. *Annals of Ulster.*
3. *Annals Tig. Annals of Ulster.*

4. *Annals of the Four Masters.*
5. *Annals Tig.*
6. *Annals Tig., Ulster, Four Masters; Song of Dermot and the Earl. Giraldus Cambrensis. Book of Leinster.* W. Carrigan, *History of the Diocese of Ossory.*
7. *Annals Tig.*
8. G. H. Orpen, *Ireland Under the Normans,* vol. 1, p. 66.
9. *Annals Tig.*
10. The *Book of Leinster* records Diarmait's defiance despite defeat. On its own the fact that he hadn't yet paid the honour price for Derbforgaill is ample testimony of his defiance, incredible though it sounds in his position.

CHAPTER 14: THE GREAT DEED DONE IN IRELAND

1. *Annals Tig.*
2. *Four Masters. Annals of Ulster,* 1166.
3. *Four Masters.*
4. The point of departure of Mac Murchada from Ireland has been a source of debate. There was no doubt in Ó Regan's mind. He names the venue since he was there. Since then it has been a question of interpretation of Ó Regan's port of departure. Ó Regan says (through *The Song of Dermot and the Earl)* that the port or point from which they left was Corcoran. This has been identified by Orpen (vol. 1, chap. 3, p. 77) as on the coast of Imokilly, south of Youghal in the county of Cork. There are other interpretations. W. H. Grattan Flood, *(Journal RSAI,* 1904, vol. 34, part 2, pp. 191, 192) declares for Corkerry at Great Island near New Ross. A theory from Richard Roche *(The Norman Invasion of Ireland,* Anvil Press, 1970) suggests a port in Bannow Bay, countyWexford.

   Orpen's Corcoran is a few miles down the Blackwater river on the Atlantic coast from Lismore and on the same side as Lismore. The man who dwelt there was the eyes and ears of Rome, legate of the pope, Gilla Críst Ua Connairche, the reforming Cistercian bishop of Lismore. The papal legate was the first witness of Diarmait's charter of foundation to the Augustinian abbey in Ferns.

   Knowing Mac Murchada there is one conclusion. Mac Murchada went to Lismore to the papal legate. I suggest that he travelled via the territory of his foster brothers, the Ua Cáellaide, west of modern New Ross. He later embarked from Corcoran down river for Bristol, with assistance from the most powerful ecclesiastic in Ireland. His son-in-law, Domnall Mór Ó Briain of Thomond, with his daughter Órlaith, may have met there too. There was no haphazard flight. Mac Murchada did little in his life that had not been carefully considered.
5. *Annals Tig., Four Masters.*
6. ibid.

CHAPTER 15: THE VITAL LINK IN BRISTOL

1. W. Dugdale, *Monasticon Anglicanum. Song of Dermot and the Earl.* G. H. Orpen, *Ireland Under the Normans,* vol. 1, chap. 3. G. T. Stokes, *Ireland and the Anglo-Norman Church.* Lecture 3.
2. *Four Masters.* E. A. Freeman, *Norman Conquest,* vol. 2. S. Seyer, *Memoirs of*

Bristol, chap. 4. J. F. Nichols & J. Taylor, *Bristol Past and Present.*

3. *Annals of Inisfallen.* This trophy was presented to Toirdelbach Ó Briain, king of Thomond, by Diarmait Mac Máel na mBó who was his foster father, in 1068, along with other treasures. A striking tribute is paid to this Irish monarch in the Welsh chronicles at the time of his death. It indicates the knowledge of the man in Wales:

> *And then Mac Máel na mBó, the most renowned and most powerful king of the Gwyddelians, was slain in a sudden onset; – the man who was terrible to his foes, friendly to his countrymen, and gentle towards pilgrims and strangers.*

CHAPTER 16: IN PURSUIT OF A MONARCH

1. *Song of Dermot and the Earl.*
2. *Giraldus Cambrensis.*
3. ibid.
4. *Song of Dermot and the Earl. Giraldus Cambrensis.*
5. *Giraldus Cambrensis.*
6. ibid.

CHAPTER 17: IN THE MARKET FOR SWORDS

1. *Giraldus Cambrensis. Song of Dermot and the Earl.*
2. *Annals Tig., Four Masters.*
3. *Song of Dermot and the Earl. Giraldus Cambrensis.*
4. ibid.
5. *Giraldus Cambrensis.*
6. G. H. Orpen, *Ireland Under the Normans*, p. 89. G. T. Stokes, *Ireland and the Anglo-Norman Church*, p. 62.
7. *Giraldus Cambrensis.*
8. ibid. *Misc. Ir. Anns.* E. Curtis, *A History of Ireland.* G. T. Stokes, *Ireland and the Anglo-Norman Church.* T. W. Moody & F. X. Martin, *Course of Irish History.* G. H. Orpen, *Ireland Under the Normans*, p. 91.
9. *Giraldus Cambrensis. Misc. Ir. Anns.*
10. The long periods spent in the dwelling and in the company of the accomplished and experienced FitzHarding gave Mac Murchada daily opportunities for conferences, briefing, assessment and strategy.
11. *Giraldus Cambrensis. Song of Dermot and the Earl. Misc. Ir. Anns.*
12. *Brut Y Tywysogion. Giraldus Cambrensis. Misc. Ir. Anns.* G. H. Orpen, *Ireland Under the Normans*, vol. 1, p. 95.
13. *Giraldus Cambrensis. Song of Dermot and the Earl.*
14. ibid.
15. *Brut Y Tywysogion.* Rolls series, 1168, p. 207. *Misc. Ir. Ans. Giraldus Cambrensis.*
16. *Giraldus Cambrensis.*
17. G. Hadden, 'Origin and Development of Wexford Town', *Journal of the Old Wexford Society*, no. 3. J. Lee & J. P. Haughton, 'Observations on Tax Assessment of Agricultural Land in County Wexford'. *Irish Journal of Agricultural Economics and Rural Sociology*, vol. 1, 1968 (An Foras Taluntais, Dublin). M. J. Gardiner & P. Ryan, 'Soils of County Wexford'. *Soil Survey Bulletin*, no. 1. (An Foras Taluntais, Dublin). In this area the Norse nevertheless identified

and farmed the best soil type pockets, e.g. Ballymagir.

18. Later killed in an abortive conflict. *Annals of the Four Masters*, 1169.
19. *Giraldus Cambrensis. Song of Dermot and the Earl.*
20. ibid.

CHAPTER 18: TO HOME

1. *Giraldus Cambrensis. Song of Dermot and the Earl. Annals of the Four Masters.*
   R. Roche, 'Roches of Wexford', *Journal of the Old Wexford Society*, no. 2. H.
   Gallwey. 'Early Norman Families', *Journal of the Old Wexford Society*, no. 3.
2. *Giraldus Cambrensis.* W. J. G. Flood, 'Glascarrig Priory', *RSAI*, 1905.
3. *Giraldus Cambrensis.* S. Ó Ceitinn, *Foras Feasa ar Éirinn.*
4. *Annals Tig. Four Masters.*
5. ibid. G. H. Orpen, *Ireland Under the Normans*, vol. 1, p. 141. Ua Ruairc is
   recorded in this extract as slaying twenty-five of Diarmait's own men plus the
   unfortunate son of the Welsh king, a factor which may have facilitated the
   recruitment of other Welsh mercenaries later.
6. *Four Masters*, 1168. The entry reads: 'Énna Mac Murchada, the royal heir of
   Leinster, was blinded by the grandson of Gilla Pátraic, lord of Ossory.'
7. *Song of Dermot and the Earl.*
8. ibid.
9. *Annals Tig., Ulster.*
10. *Annals Tig., Four Masters.* D. F. Gleeson, *History of the Diocese of Killaloe.* part
    2. *Misc. Ir. Anns.*
11. *Giraldus Cambrensis. Song of Dermot and the Earl.* L. Hyman, *The Jews of
    Ireland.* Chap 1. p. 4.
12. G. T. Stokes, *Ireland and the Anglo-Norman Church.* Enquires to any county
    Wexford fisherman or sailor.
13. *Giraldus Cambrensis.*

CHAPTER 19: THE HELP ARRIVES

1. *Annals of the Four Masters, Tig. Misc. Ir. Anns. Giraldus Cambrensis. Song of
   Dermot and the Earl.* W. Carrigan, *History of the Diocese of Ossory.* P. H. Hore,
   History of the Town and County of Wexford. It is certain that Mac Murchada
   had waiting observers. No newly arrived Flemish or Norman messenger
   could risk a strange land and route.
2. *Giraldus Cambrensis.*
3. ibid. *Song of Dermot and the Earl.*
4. *Giraldus Cambrensis.*
5. P. H. Hore, *History of the Town and County of Wexford.* G. Redmond, *Waterford
   and SEI Archaeological Society*, vol. 5, p. 242.
6. P. H. Hore, *History of the Town and County of Wexford.* N. Furlong. 'Town that
   Died' (Clonmines), *Journal of the Old Wexford Society*, no. 1. The registration
   number of the Viking hoard discovered near the Black Castle (FitzHenrys)
   in Clonmines is W5, National Museum of Ireland. *Giraldus Cambrensis.*
7. G. Hadden, 'Origin and Development of Wexford', *Journal of the Old Wexford
   Society*, no. 1. *Giraldus Cambrensis.*
8. *Song of Dermot and the Earl. Giraldus Cambrensis.*
9. G. Hadden, 'Origin and Development of Wexford', *Journal of the Old Wexford*

Society, nos. 1, 2. P. H. Hore, *History of the Town and County of Wexford. Giraldus Cambrensis. Song of Dermot and the Earl.*

10. P. H. Hore, *History of the Town and County of Wexford.* 'Report of Brother Alan to Abbot of Buildwas, 1182', vol. 3. G. H. Orpen, *Ireland Under the Normans,* vol. 1, p. 324. G. Hadden, 'Origin and Development of Wexford', *Journal of the Old Wexford Society,* no. 3.

CHAPTER 20: HELL TO OSRAIGE

1. *Giraldus Cambrensis.*
2. *Annals Tig.,* 1165. G. H. Orpen, *Ireland Under the Normans,* pp. 69–70.
3. *Giraldus Cambrensis. Song of Dermot and the Earl. Annals of Clonmacnoise.* W. Carrigan, *History of the Diocese of Ossory.* The pass of Gowran is the most likely.
4. *Giraldus Cambrensis.*
5. W. Carrigan, *History of the Diocese of Ossory. Song of Dermot and the Earl.* G. H. Orpen, *Ireland Under the Normans, p.* 161.
6. *Song of Dermot and the Earl. Giraldus Cambrensis.* W. Carrigan, *History of the Diocese of Ossory.*
7. *Song of Dermot and the Earl.*
8. *Song of Dermot and the Earl.* W. Carrigan, *History of the Diocese of Ossory.* G. H. Orpen, *Ireland Under the Normans.*

CHAPTER 21: A SON FOR THE HIGH KING'S DAUGHTER

1. *Song of Dermot and the Earl.* G. H. Orpen, *Ireland Under the Normans,* p. 167. *Giraldus Cambrensis.* Giraldus, the historian, was given his comprehensive account of the Normans in Ireland years after the events by his uncle Robert FitzStephen and many others who lived through the early landings. He never mentions de Prendergast except by allusion. (See chapter 5, p. 196). In one brief passage he echoes both Robert FitzStephen's disgust at de Prendergast's desertion but also conveys some of the intensity of FitzStephen's own loyalty to Mac Murchada – and there is the significant mention of the oath of fealty to Diarmait. 'Meanwhile Diarmait in the time of his utmost need found that he had very few firm supporters except FitzStephen and his men. Some of his other reed-like friends abandoning his cause, and withdrawing privately from his standard, and the rest openly joining his enemies, and so breaking their oaths of fealty to him.'
2. *Four Masters. Annals Tig. Giraldus Cambrensis.*
3. *Song of Dermot and the Earl.*
4. *Giraldus Cambrensis.*
5. This prelate, whose loyalty to Diarmait repeats itself, is not mentioned by name. Giraldus, himself a senior clergyman, attributes peace to 'good men, with the assistance of divine mercy'. With the confrontation so close to Ferns and so crucial in its effects it is certain that Diarmait's bishop, no stranger to negotiations, was there – and if he was, he was an active intermediary with the Mac Murchada interest uppermost in his mind.
6. *Annals Tig.* P. Walsh, 'Kings of Meath', *IER,* Jan. to June 1941. The name Donnchad Chennselaig Ua Cáellaide suggests that the assassination was planned and proposed in Ferns by Diarmait Mac Murchada.

Chapter 22: The Restoration in Leinster

1. *Song of Dermot and the Earl. Giraldus Cambrensis.*
2. *Song of Dermot and the Earl.* W. Carrigan, *History of the Diocese of Ossory.*
3. *Song of Dermot and the Earl.* P. H. Hore, vol. 5. W. Carrigan. *History of the Diocese of Ossory.*
4. *Giraldus Cambrensis.*
5. ibid. *Annals Tig*, 1170, which recorded that 'Mac Murchada received the kingship of the foreigners of Leinster'.
6. *Annals Tig*, 1170. *Four Masters.* From Mac Murchada's point of view the only thing wrong with Ua Briain's tactics was his timing. Mac Murchada was not ready. *Giraldus Cambrensis.*
7. *Giraldus Cambrensis.*
8. ibid.

Chapter 23: Strongbow

1. *Giraldus Cambrensis.*
2. ibid. Gervase of Canterbury. *Historical Works*, vol. 1, p. 234.
3. *Song of Dermot and the Earl. Giraldus Cambrensis.*
4. *Song of Dermot. Giraldus Cambrensis.* Ua Faéláin, king of Déisi now figures in the Waterford harbour area of operations. He was with the Osraige and Waterford attack on Dun Donnell and also in the siege of Waterford. His life was spared by the arrival in Waterford of Diarmait Mac Murchada. Another contingent to join the Osraige men at Baginbun were from Uí Drona, a territory annexed from Uí Chennselaig and bestowed on Osraige at Diarmait's humiliation in 1166. G. H. Orpen, *Ireland Under the Normans*, pp. 135–88.
5. This was the real name of one of our major authorities who used the pen name 'Giraldus Cambrensis' or 'Gerald of Wales'. G. T. Stokes gives a summary in his work *Ireland and the Anglo-Norman Church.*
6. *Giraldus Cambrensis.*
7. There were penalties paid by some who did leave with Strongbow. (*Pipe Roll* 1170). G. T. Stokes, *Ireland and the Anglo-Norman Church.* William of Newburgh, *Chron. Reign Henry II*, vol. 1, p. 168. L. Hyman, chap. 1, p. 4.
8. *Giraldus Cambrensis. Song of Dermot and the Earl. Annals Tig., Four Masters.* The Irish annals thought lightly of the new foreign group. They do not clarify the dates of the landings or the dates of the capture of Wexford and Waterford. There is a school of thought which maintains that Giraldus Cambrensis was given the wrong dates for Raymond's landing at Baginbun and later Strongbow's at Passage. But his informants were his relatives and the memory of that atrocious little campaign would not have diminished.

Chapter 24: The Norsemen's Atlantic Base

1. Diarmait's great predecessor, the only Uí Chennselaig ruler to have previously claimed the kingship of Ireland, took and plundered Waterford in 1037 but 'it would appear that he had taken advantage of a state of civil strife in the city and may have been called in as an ally on one side'. Donncha Ó Corráin, 'The Career of Diarmait Mac Máel na mBó', *Journal of the Old Wexford Society*, nos. 3, 4. C. Smith, Waterford. p. 169.

2. *Four Masters, Annals Tig. Giraldus Cambrensis.*
3. ibid. *Song of Dermot and the Earl. Misc. Ir. Anns.* G. T. Stokes, *Ireland and the Anglo-Norman Church,* pp. 98–99.
4. *Giraldus Cambrensis.*
5. *Song of Dermot and the Earl. Giraldus Cambrensis.*
6. Askulv, the ruler of Norse Dublin, has had his name recorded in several ways: Askulf, Asgall, Hesculf, Esculf, Hasculfus. He was the son of Raghnal, the son of Turcall (*Four Masters,* 1170) For an account of the coins of his period see J. Lindsay's *Coinage of Ireland,* p. 17. *Song of Dermot and the Earl. Giraldus Cambrensis.*
7. *Annals Tig., Ulster,* 1170. *Four Masters. Giraldus Cambrensis. Song of Dermot and the Earl.* Diarmait's son-in-law, Domnall Mór Ua Briain, also contributed to the strategy. He and the Dal Cais were in open war against Ruaidrí. (*Annals Tig.*).
8. *Giraldus Cambrensis. Song of Dermot and the Earl.*
9. ibid.
10. *Four Masters. Annals Tig. Misc. Ir. Anns. Giraldus Cambrensis.*
11. ibid. 'They made a raiding invasion into Tír Briuin after that and took away many people and cattle to their camp.' (*Four Masters*). Tír Briuin was in the extremity of Ua Ruairc's Bréifne.
12. *Annals Tig.*
13. ibid. *Four Masters.*

CHAPTER 25: A CORPSE FOR A KING
1. *Giraldus Cambrensis.* Giraldus puts flowery speeches into the mouths of those he describes, a lot of it 'uttered' in the heat of battle in his own imaginative prose. These quotations from him, however, are so close to the characteristics of the men to whom he ascribes them as to be acceptable. Mac Murchada's 'Ancient Inheritance' refers to the conquests of his predecessor, Diarmait Mac Maél na mBó.
2. *Annals of Ulster, Tig., Four Masters* (1170). *Giraldus Cambrensis.*
3. ibid.

CHAPTER 26: THE DEATH OF DIARMAIT THE KING
1. *The Song of Dermot and the Earl* is the only source which mentions his winter-long illness, apart from the *Four Masters,* who, centuries after his death, ascribe the end to him quoted in our introduction, all details of which are in marked contrast to the contemporary notices of his death in the *Book of Leinster.* Of the actual cause of death there have been a few theories. All of them, unfortunately, are conjecture. In the edition of the *Four Masters* edited by Geraghty there is a note on Diarmait's condition to this effect ... 'it is supposed to have been the *morbis pedicularis* of medical writers' – the well-known soldiers' complaint of lice occupation with their capability as disease carriers. Hitherto undetected VD has been proposed. R. Roche's suggestion (*The Norman Invasion of Ireland,* Anvil Books) is that he may have died from leprosy contracted from the Normans who had been on the Crusades. However neither *Giraldus Cambrensis, Song of Dermot and the Earl,* nor any other contemporary Irish annals mentions any of these remarkable causes

of death, so we are left with an open verdict. The one thing of which we are certain is the abrupt disappearance of Diarmait Mac Murchada from the scene after the slaying of his hostages at the insistence of Ua Ruairc. No one has yet concluded the possibility of coronary thrombosis or a stroke of paralysis as a result of the violent stress visited upon him.

2. *Giraldus Cambrensis*. The Norse had been extensively involved in this enterprise which had Bristol as its centre.

3. *Four Masters. Giraldus Cambrensis*. On Diarmait's illness also, Mac Carthaig of Desmond made strenuous efforts to eliminate the Norman garrison in Waterford. Strongbow had to fly there from Dublin on 1 October.

4. J. F. O'Doherty, 'Historical Criticism of Song of Dermot', *Irish Historical Studies*, vol. 1, no. 1.

5. P. H. Hore, *History of the Town and County of Wexford*, vol. 6.

CHAPTER 27: THE AFTERMATH OF DIARMAIT

1. *Book of Leinster*, Regnal lists LL, 311, etc. *Four Masters. Misc. Ir. Annals*, 1172. 2. G. H. Orpen, *Ireland Under the Normans*, vol. 1, pp. 222–3. P. H. Hore, *History of the Town and County of Wexford*, vol. 6, p. 4. Giraldus, referring to Murtough, describes him as 'Murchertach Kenceleiae Principis ...' F. J. Byrne, *Rise of the Uí Neill*, pp. 8–9.

2. *Song of Dermot and the Earl*. P. H. Hore, *History of the Town and County of Wexford*, Ferns, vol. 6.

3. *Annals Tig., Ulster, Four Masters*.

4. *Annals Four Masters, Tig., Loch Ce, Ulster*, 1186.

5. *Annals Tig., Ulster*, 1171.

6. W. Carrigan, *History of the Diocese of Ossory*, vol. 1, p. 7.

7. F. X. Martin, 'The Anglo-Norman Invasion', *Course of Irish History*.

8. ibid.

9. *Giraldus Cambrensis*, chapters 8–14, book 2. After Domnall Ua Briain's chess work on Raymond le Gros, Henry remarked. 'The attack of Limerick was bold adventure, its relief a greater; but its evacuation was an act of pure wisdom.'

10. *Song of Dermot and the Earl*. In addition to Domnall Caémánach Mac Murchada there was only Ó Ragallaig of Tír Briuin in Bréifne and Amlaib Ua Gairbith of Uí Felmeda whose area was near Rathvilly in county Carlow. At this point Muirchertach, Diarmait's nephew and successor, reached his major influence for he succeeded in rallying wide support to curb the mercenaries. That again is another story, but it also included the hiring of more mercenaries, this time the Norse. *Annals Tig.*, 1171. *Giraldus Cambrensis*.

11. The number of occasions on which it is stated that Strongbow succeeded Diarmait as 'king of Leinster' is bewildering in view of the fact that no such succession is recorded or recognised by any of the reputable contemporary sources from the side whose sole property it was to elect and bestow legal power, namely the Irish side. The power to rule a sub-kingdom, or all Ireland, even by the sword, was granted only to the elected kings from the families whose hereditary right, duty and life's function in society was to rule. The right to rule could not be claimed by an ecclesiastic, or a judge, or professor no matter how popular or accomplished; still less by a hired Norman French bankrupt however capable, unfortunate or lovable a man he may have been.

12. The Hook Peninsula and the former Norse, harsh lands granted by Diarmait Mac Murchada. These included, as we have seen, Fotharta Laghin or Forth, the tributary state of the foreigners south of Wexford town. G. Hadden, *Journal of the Old Wexford Society*, no. 3.

13. *Giraldus Cambrensis*. G. H. Orpen, *Ireland Under the Normans*.

14. J. F. O'Doherty, 'St Laurence O'Toole', *IER* (July-Dec. 1937), pp. 600–11. W. L. Warren. 'The Interpretation of Twelfth-Century Irish History,' *Historical Studies*, VII.

15. *Pipe Roll 18th Henry II*. G. H. Orpen, *Ireland Under the Normans*, p. 257. *Giraldus Cambrensis*.

16. *Annals Tig.* (1171), *Loch Ce, Ulster*, the *Four Masters* do not record a 'submission to Henry'.

17. Henry spent two days in Lismore, a fortress not of military but of unquestionable ecclesiastical and political power. *Giraldus Cambrensis*.

18. ibid. De Lacy had not taken part in Mac Murchada's campaign at all, as Strongbow had. *Song of Dermot and the Earl*.

19. G. H. Orpen, *Ireland Under the Normans*, vol. 1, p. 273.

20. P. H. Hore, *History of the Town and County of Wexford*, Wexford town vol. *Giraldus Cambrensis*. Henry confirmed, or allowed his subjects hired by Mac Murchada to retain the territories granted to them in fee by Mac Murchada – or disallowed them, as in the case of Robert FitzStephen. These territories included the former Viking enclaves of Leinster. The exception was the grant of Meath to de Lacy, a grant regarded and resisted by Meath's ruling family as any grant in the previous century. A grant of land was only as permanent as the strength of the grantee's sword.

21. Graphic description of situation from Strongbow's point of view and Norse resurgence in *Giraldus Cambrensis*, book 2, chap. 1, p. 255..

22. *Annals of the Four Masters, Tig*.

23. F. X. Martin, 'Anglo-Norman Invasion', *Course of Irish History*. Due to the meticulous Norman records, the Normans appear larger than life. To the Irish of 1169 they were not as remarkable as the Norsemen, either in fortification, endurance or numbers. The Norse town of Wexford could raise an army of 2,000 men. And they had been in Ireland for 300 years by 1170. Therefore, they presented an enduring foreign presence to Irish eyes in 1169.

24. B. O'Dwyer, *Conspiracy of Mellifont*.

25. Note the power of the Mac Murchada circa 1540. P. H. Hore, *History of the Town and County of Wexford*, vol. 6. pp. 16–18. RSAI, V. 43, p. 57. Sixteenth-century Mac Murchada – 'Rex Totius Lageniae'. See *Mac Murchada Caemanach*, Genealogical Office, Department of the Taoiseach, Dublin 2.

26. P. H. Hore, *History of the Town and County of Wexford*, Ferns, vol. 6. British Museum, Cat. 34, 47. Described as follows: '17,335. Fifteenth century. Donat Mac Murchada, king of Leinster. Red wax or composition from the matrix 25/8 inch. Within a quatrefoil spandrils each charge with a small cinquefoil, a shield of arms (field replenished with sprigs); in chief a lion passant, in base two crescents. Supported on either side by a lion rampant, reguardant, tail coward. Upheld above and below by a demi-angel, winged and draped.'

27. W. F. Butler, 'Ormonde and Mac Murrough, King of Leinster, 1475 Treaty', *RSAI*, vol. 43, p. 57.

BIBLIOGRAPHY
(1974 Edition)

MANUSCRIPT SOURCES
Royal Irish Academy, Dublin:
Book of Armagh, Fac. and MSS.
Book of Ballymote, Fac. and MSS.
Book of Genealogies, Fac.
Vienna:
Dominikanerkloster, Konventsbibliothek, Cod. Nr. 70/291. Folio 96V, Nr. 140 und 141.

PRINTED SOURCES
Annals of Clonmacnoise, edited by D. Murphy (Dublin 1896).
Annals of Inisfallen, edited by S. MacAirt (Dublin 1951).
Annals of the Four Masters, edited by J. O'Donovan, 7 vols. (Dublin 1848–51).
Annals of Loch Ce, edited by W. A. Hennessy, 2 vols. (Dublin 1939).
The Annals of Tigernach, edited by W. Stokes. *Revue celtique* 16–18 (Paris 1895–97).
Annals of Ulster, edited by W. M. Hennessy & B. MacCarthy, 4 vols. (Dublin 1887–1901).
Bernard, Abbot of Clairvaux. *Patrologia Latina,* edited by Jacques Paul Migne, letter 361 (1844–45).
Book of Leinster, edited by Best, Bergin & O'Brien, 7 vols. (Dublin 1965).
Book of Rights, translation and notes, John O'Donovan (Dublin 1847).
Brut Y Tywysogion, edited by J. Williams ab Ithel (London 1860).
Campion, Edmund, *History of Ireland,* (Oxford 1571. Reprint 1809).
Chronicum Scotorum, edited by W. M. Hennessy, R.S. (1866).
Cogadh Gaedhel re Gallaibh. (Wars of the Gael with the Gaill), trans. J. H. Todd, R.S. (1867).
Crith Gablach, edited by D. A. Binchy (Dublin 1941).
Dugdale, W., *Monastican Anglicanum,* edited by Dugdale (1846).
Gardiner, M. J. & P. Ryan, 'Soils of County Wexford'. *Soil Survey Bulletin,* no. 1. (An Foras Taluntais, Dublin).
Gervase of Canterbury, *Historical Works,* edited by W. Stokes (1879–80).
Giraldus Cambrensis, *The Historical Works of Giraldus Cambrensis* London & New York 1892).
The Great Roll of the Pipe for the 14th *Year of Henry II.* (London 1890).
The Great Roll of the Pipe for the 15th *Year of Henry II.* (London 1890).
The Great Roll of the Pipe for the 16th *Year of Henry II.* (London 1892).
The Great Roll of the Pipe for the 17th *Year of Henry II.* (London 1893).
The Great Roll of the Pipe for the 18th *Year of Henry II.* (London 1894).
Lee, J. & Haughton, J. P., 'Observations on Tax Assessment of Agricultural Land in County Wexford'. *Irish Journal of Agricultural Economics and Rural Sociology,* vol. 1, 1968 (An Foras Taluntais, Dublin).
Miscellaneous Irish Annals, edited by S. Ó hInnse (Dublin 1947).
Pontificia Hibernica, edited by M. P. Sheehy (Dublin 1962–65).

Registrum Prioratus Omnium Sanctorum Juxta Dublin, edited by R. Butler (1845).

Salisbury, John of, *Historia Pontificalis,* edited by M. Chibnall (1956).

Metalogicon, edited by C. C. J. Webb, 4 vols. (1929).

Song of Dermot and the Earl, trans. G. H. Orpen (Oxford).

Trias Thaumaturga, edited by John Colgan (Louvain 1647).

Veterum Epistolarum Hibernicarum Sylloge, edited by J. Ussher (Dublin 1632).

William of Newburg, *Chron, Reigns Stephen, Henry II, Richard I,* edited by R. Howlett, R.S. (1889).

MODERN WORKS

Butler, W. F., 'Ormonde and Mac Murrough, King of Leinster Treaty 1475' *Journal of the Royal Society of Antiquaries of Ireland,* vol. 43.

Byrne, F. J., *The Rise of the Uí Neill and the High Kingship of Ireland* (National University of Ireland, 1969).

Carrigan, William, *The History and Antiquities of the Diocese of Ossory* (Dublin 1905).

Ceitinn, Seatrun, *Foras Feasa ar Éirinn,* Irish Texts Society (London 1908).

Cleirig, Arthur Ua, *The History of Ireland to the Coming of Henry II* (London 1908).

Colmcille, Fr, OCSO, *The Story of Mellifont* (1958).

Curtis, Edmund, *A History of Ireland* (London 1936).

Dalton, J. P., 'St Vauk of Carne'. *The Past,* (Enniscorthy 1921).

Douglas, David C., *The Norman Achievements,* (London 1969).

Farrow, John, *Pageant of the Popes* (St Paul 1955).

Flood, W. J. Grattan, *History of the Diocese of Ferns* (Waterford 1916). 'Corkeran' (1904). 'Glascarrig Priory' (1905). *Journal of the Roal Society of Antiquaries of Ireland.*

Freeman, Edward August, *The History of the Norman Conquest of England* (Oxford 1867–79).

Furlong, Nicholas, 'The Immediate Predecessors of Dermot Mac Murrough, Dermot Mac Énna Mac Murrough 1115–1117, Énna Mac Donncha Mac Murrough 1117–1126', *Journal of the Old Wexford Society,* no. 4, '1400 Years on Guard'. (Hook) *Biatas,* vol. 17, no. 6, 1963.

Gallwey, Hubert, 'Some Early Norman Families in County Wexford', *Journal of the Old Wexford Society,* no. 3.

Ginnell, Laurence, *The Brehon Laws,* 3rd edition (Dublin).

Gleeson, Dermot F., *A History of the Diocese of Killaloe,* part 2 (Dublin 1961).

Gwynn, A. & R. N. Hancock, *Mediaeval Religious Houses in Ireland,* (London 1970).

Gwynn, Aubrey, 'The Centenary of the Synod of Kells'. *Irish Ecclesiastical Record,* March-April 1952. 'The Twelfth-Century Reform', *A History of Irish Catholicism,* edited by Patrick J. Corish.

Hadden, George, 'The Origin and Development of Wexford Town', *Journal of the Old Wexford Society,* nos. 1–3.

Hogan, E., 'Tricha Cet'. *Proc. RIA,* vol. 38.

Hore, Philip H., *History of the Town and County of Wexford.* 6 vols. (London 1911).

Hyman, Louis, *The Jews of Ireland* (Shannon 1972).

Joyce, P. W., *Social History of Ancient Ireland* (London & Dublin 1908).

Kelly, Matthew, 'The Synod of Cashel 1172'. *Dissertations on Irish History* (Dublin 1864).

Lindsay, John, *Coinage of Ireland* (Cork 1839).

MacEvedy, Colin, *Atlas of Mediaeval History*, vol. 2 (London).

MacGearailt, Gearoid, *Celts and Normans* (Dublin 1969).

MacNeill, Eoin, *Phases of Irish History* (Dublin 1919).

Moody, T. W. & F. X. Martin, *The Course of Irish History*, (Cork 1967).

Muir, Ramsay, *Historical Atlas*, edited by H. Fullard & R. F. Treharne, (London 1963).

Murphy, Patrick, *Our Lady's Island, Wexford, in History and Legend* (Wexford 1963).

Nicholls, J. F. & Taylor, J., *Bristol Past and Present*, (Bristol 1881).

Norman, E. R. & St Joseph, J. K. S., *The Early Development of Irish Society: Evidence of Aerial Photography*, (Cambridge 1969).

Ó Corráin, Donncha, 'The Career of Diarmait Mac Máel na mBó, King of Leinster', *Journal of the Old Wexford Society*, nos. 3, 4.

Ó Cuív, Brian, 'Ireland in the Eleventh and Twelfth Centuries'. *Course of Irish History*.

O'Curry, Eugene, *Lectures on the Manuscript Materials of Ancient Irish History* (London 1861).

O'Doherty, J. F., *Laurentius von Dublin und das irische Normannentum*, (Diss. Munich 1933), 'Saint Laurence O'Toole and the Anglo-Norman Invasion'. *Irish Ecclesiastical Record* 50 (1937) and 51 (1938). 'Historical criticism of the Song of Dermot and the Earl'. *Irish Historical Studies*, vol. 1, no. 1 (1938).

O'Donovan, John, *Ordnance Survey Letters Relating to County Wexford*, 1840 (Wexford County Library).

O'Dwyer, Barry W., *The Conspiracy of Mellifont*, 1216–31 (Dublin 1970).

O'Hanlon, John, *The Life of St Laurence O'Toole* (Dublin 1857).

Ó Huíginn, Tadgh Dall, *The Bardic Poems of Tadgh Dall Ó Huíginn*, edited by Eleanor Knott (Irish Texts Society).

Orpen, G. H., *Ireland Under the Normans* (Oxford 1911).

O'Toole, P. L., *History of the Clan O'Toole and-other Leinster Septs*, (Dublin 1890).

Otway-Ruthven, A. J., *A History of Medieval Ireland* (London 1967).

Redmond, Gabriel O'C., 'History and Topography of the Tower of Hook'. *Proc. Waterford and South-East of Ireland Archaeological Society*, vol. 5.

Richards, Melville, 'Irish Settlements in South-West Wales', *RSAI*, vol. XC, part 2.

Roche, Richard, 'The Roches of Wexford', *Journal of the Old Wexford Society*, no. 2.

Ryan, John, *Toirdelbach Ua Conchobair*, (NUI 1966). 'Brian Bóruma, King of Ireland'. *North Munster Studies*. (Limerick 1967) 'The Early History of Leinster', *The Past*, vol. 4 (Enniscorthy 1948).

Seyer, Samuel, *Memoirs of Bristol* (Bristol 1821–23).

Shearman, John F., 'Early Kings of Ossory', *Kilkenny Archaeological Journal*, vol. 4.

Smith, Charles, *The Ancient and Present State of the County and City of Waterford*. (Dublin 1774).

Stokes, G. T., *Ireland and the Anglo-Norman Church*, London (1892).

Walsh, Paul, 'Leinster States and Kings', *Irish Ecclesiastical Record* (1939). 'The Kings of Meath', *IER* (1941). 'Sir Mulmory M. Swiny, Chieftain (1596–1630)', *IER*, (1938).